THE INSEPARABLE CONNECTION BETWEEN A SINNER'S HAVING PART WITH CHRIST, AND BEING WASHED BY HIM: OR, THE MYSTERY OF SANCTIFICATION BY CHRIST, OPENED UP.

Several sermons, preached at Ettrick, in the year 1728.

N. B. The first Sermon was preached immediately before the celebration of the Lord's Supper, August 18, 1728; and the others on some subsequent Lord's days.

JOHN xiii. 8.

If I wash thee not, thou hast no part with me.

THESE words are Christ's answer to Peter refusing to let Christ wash his feet. No doubt it was a kind of modesty, reverence, and humility, that put Peter on this peremptory refusal of Christ's astonishing kind offer. But all is not gold that glitters. There is much of this bastard humility in the world, whereby people refuse Christ's offers, and put them away from them, with a very good grace, and great respect to the Lord Christ, as they think. Christ comes to sinners in the gospel, and offers to wash them from their pollution: But will they offer a foul defiled soul to God Almighty, the infinitely holy Saviour, to be washed by him? No; they think they know more of their own sinfulness and unworthiness, and of Christ's greatness and holiness, than that comes to. And so they affront him, under a pretence of honouring him.

There are three characters of this false humility.

1. It condemns the generation of the righteous, who came all to Christ, at his command, to be washed by him, receiving it with admiration of his condescension. The other disciples, no doubt, were struck with amazement at Christ's coming to wash their feet: but true humility took Christ's will for law and right, and makes them silently yield themselves to the Lord. But Peter's behaviour condemns them, as rude and disrespectful, vers. 5, 6, "After that, he poureth water into a bason, and began to wash the disciples' feet, and to wipe them with the towel wherewith he was girded. Then cometh he to Simon Peter: and Peter saith unto him, Lord, dost thou wash my feet?

2. It keeps Christ at a distance, and so proceeds not from faith, but unbelief, ver. 6. No doubt, when Christ stretched out his hand to wash Peter's feet, he drew them in quickly to him; and shewed by his deeds, as well as his words, that he had no mind that Christ's

fair hand should come on them. So folk, under a sense of sinfulness, may flee from Christ, while he follows them.

3. It argues a heart not duly humbled; and so it is but accursed pride under the vail of a shew of humility. (1.) Carnal wisdom and reason has the ascendant, and will not bow to divine revelation: vers. 7, 8, "Jesus answered and said unto him, What I do thou knowest not now; but thou shalt know hereafter. Peter saith unto him, Thou shalt never wash my feet. Jesus answered him, "If I wash thee not, thou hast no part with me." Let the gospel of God's grace be delivered never so plain, they will not give over measuring divine mysteries by their carnal reason. (2.) Insensibleness and self-conceit prevails. Peter doubtless thought either that his feet needed no washing, but that they might be borne with even in Christ's presence, as they were; or, if they did, he would wash them himself. So he is peremptory in his refusal. And this lies at bottom in that false humility: either they think they are not so very polluted, but that they may be borne with; or else, that they will wash themselves clean before they come to Christ.

In the text our Lord gives Peter a word that brings him down in a moment from all his heights, and makes him not only content, but earnest to be washed all over by Christ, without pretending to wipe off one spot off himself by himself: "If I wash thee not, thou hast no part with me. Ver. 9, Simon Peter saith unto him, Lord, not my feet only, but also my hands and my head." This word strikes Peter to the heart, "If I wash thee not, thou hast no part with me." Q. d. Peter, no washing by me, no part with me to salvation. Washing by me, and part with me, you nor no man shall ever be able to separate in your cases. Have the one, have the other; want the one, and upon heaven's truth you want the other."

I think it is an insipid question here, why so severe a threatening for refusing so small a thing? For Christ says not, if I wash not thy feet, thou shalt have no part with me; but simply, "If I wash thee not, thou hast no part with me," in the present time. Neither could it be drawn to the washing of the feet, if the questionists did not first suppose a change of the tense the Holy Ghost useth, which is not at least without necessity to be admitted. (Gr.) If I washed thee not, or, if I have not washed thee, thou hast no part with me. Q. d. Peter, if you belong to me, I have done more for you, than to wash your feet with water; I have washed you with my blood: if you have taken that vastly costlier washing off my hand, why refuse you this? If I have not so washed you, you have no part with me; for none have part with me, but those whom I so wash."

The words then bear an inseparable connection betwixt two

things in the case of sinners, standing and falling together. (1.) The washing of them by Christ, to wit, from their sins, Rev. i. 5. (2.) Their having part with him, partaking of his saving benefits, being joint heirs of heaven with him. Compare Deut. xiv. 27, "And the Levite that is within thy gates, thou shalt not forsake him: for he hath no part nor inheritance with thee." The Scripture knows no part sinners can have of salvation or of heaven, but with Christ: Acts iv. 12, "Neither is their salvation in any other: for there is none other name under heaven given among men whereby we must be saved." They that miss their part with Christ, there is but another side where their part will fall: Rev. xxi. 8, "But the fearful, and unbelieving, and the abominable, and murderers, and whoremongers, and sorcerers, and idolaters, and all liars, shall have their part in the lake which burneth with fire and brimstone: which is the second death." Now, if a sinner either be not washed at all, or be washed only with the nitre and soap of his own faithless endeavours and reformation; if he be not washed by Christ; he has no part with him, he is none of his; he is in a state of death and destruction lying ready to be cast out as an abominable thing, into the unclean place, the stinking lake.

The relation betwixt these two, is, the former is a necessary consequent of the latter; and therefore is held forth as a necessary evidence of it. All that have saving part with Christ are washed by him: therefore, if Christ hath not washed thee, thou hast no saving part with him.

The doctrine deducible from the words is as follows.

DOCTRINE A sinner's having any saving part with Christ, and his being washed by Christ, from his sin, are simply and absolutely inseparable.

In discoursing from this doctrine shortly at the time, I shall,
I. Consider a sinner's having part with Christ.
II. His being washed by Christ.
III. The inseparableness of the two.
IV. Improve the doctrine.

I. The first thing to be spoken to, is, A sinner's having part with Christ. And this we take in two things.

1. His being of Christ's mystical body, through union with him: 1 Cor. xii. 12, 13, "For as the body is one, and hath many members, and all the members of that one body, being many, are one body: so also is Christ. For by one Spirit are we all baptized into one body, whether we be Jews or Gentiles, whether we be bond or free; and have been all made to drink into one Spirit." There are

but two general corporations of mankind on earth, heaven, and hell: the corporation of the first and fallen Adam, who has diffused all manner of pollution and defilement over those that are his, not to be washed off by human art; and of this society we are all by nature members: the corporation of the Second Adam, Christ, who cleanses and purifies all that are his, from that pollution and defilement; for the latter is raised out of the former. See the two, 1 John v. 19, "And we know that we are of God, and the whole world lieth in wickedness." 2 Cor. vi. 17, Wherefore come out from among them, and be ye separate, saith the Lord, and touch not the unclean thing; and I will receive you." Now, if ye are not washed by Christ, ye belong not to the Second Adam's corporation; ye belong not to Christ.

2. The sinner's having communion with Christ in his saving benefits, partaking of them in fellowship with him: 1 John i. 3, "That which we have seen and heard, declare we unto you, that ye also may have fellowship with us: and truly our fellowship is with the Father, and with his son Jesus Christ." All salvation is in Christ; so that they who have part with him, are complete in him, Col. ii. 9, 10. And salvation is in him exclusively to all other, Acts iv. 12. Now, if ye are not washed by Christ, ye have no communion with him in his saving benefits, no part in his salvation, and so none in salvation at all. Christ has a righteousness fully answering the law's demands; it is so broad a white raiment, that it covers all his people, partaking with him in it, Rom. iii. 22. But if he wash you not, ye have no part in it. He has taken out a new right to God, as his God, and all his people partake with him in it: Rom. viii. 17, "And if children then heirs; heirs of God, and joint heirs with Christ." John xx. 17, "I ascend unto my Father, and your Father, and to my God, and your God." But if Christ wash you not ye have no part, he is not your God

II. The next thing to be spoken to, is, The sinner's being washed by Christ. This is inseparable from his having part with Christ, and is the privilege of all, and only those who have part with him. Concerning this washing I offer these particulars.

1. There is a filthiness in sin, whereby the soul is polluted and defiled before the Lord. This is supposed in the washing from it: Ezek. xxxvi. 25, "Then will I sprinkle clean water upon you, and ye shall be clean: from all your filthiness, and from all your idols will I cleanse you." Sin does not only make the sinner guilty, but filthy and abominable. It is the abominable thing that God hates, Jer. xliv. 4. filth itself, Is. iv. 4. This filthiness of sin lies in its contrariety to the holiness of God expressed in his law. Holiness

is the glory of God, and the beauty of the soul, Exod. xv. 11; sin the deformity and filthiness of it. Hence,

1*st*, It makes the sinner loathsome before God, that he cannot look on him, but with abhorrence; and with such abhorrence as one looks upon a thing he has a natural antipathy at, Zech. xi. 8, "My soul loathed them." Hab. i. 13, "Thou art of purer eyes than to behold evil, and canst not look on iniquity." Psal. v. 4, "For thou art not a God that hath pleasure in wickedness: neither shall evil dwell with thee."

2*dly*, It fills the soul with shame before God. I mean not that holy shame that proceeds from a joint view of sin's loathsomeness, and God's pardoning grace in Christ; that is a fruit of the Spirit, Ezek. xvi. 60, 61, "I will establish unto thee an everlasting covenant. Then thou shalt remember thy ways, and be ashamed." But I mean a natural shame, whereby the sinner, obliged to fix his eyes on God's holiness, and seeing his own unlikeness to him, his countenance falls, he is damped, and filled with dread and horror, and therefore labours to make away out of his presence; as Adam did, Gen. iii. 10, "I heard thy voice," said he to the Lord, "in the garden: and I was afraid, because I was naked; and I hid myself." Now, unwashed sinners are filthy all over.

(1.) Their nature is filthy, Psal. xiv. 3, "They are all gone aside, they are altogether become filthy: there is none that doth good, no not one." Sin has spread its defilement over all the faculties of their souls, and over all the members of their bodies: Tit. i. 15, "Unto them that are defiled, and unbelieving, is nothing pure; but even their mind and conscience is defiled." Their very bodies, however perfumed and adorned, are filthy before God with spiritual filth cleaving to them, Heb. x. 22.

(2.) Their life and conversation is filthy, 2 Pet. ii. 7. Their daily walk is a heaping new filth upon their already filthy souls. Their habitual filthiness produces still actual filthiness, as the poisoned spring sends forth poisonous streams, Psal. xiv. 1.

2. Christ has them all to wash who get part in him. Hence the redeemed church sings praises to him that loved them, and washed them from their sins in his own blood, Rev. i. 5. They come to him in their pollution, and are washed by him; they come to him defiled all over, in the defilement of their nature, and of their life, that they may be washed; and coming to him by faith, it is done, Ezek. xvi. 8, 9; Rom. iv. 5; 2 Cor. v. 17. How can it be otherwise? for they cannot wash themselves before they come. Is it possible for people to wash, before they come to the waters? or to bathe before they come into the laver?

3. All those who take part with him by faith, he washes with his blood from their sin, Heb. xii. 24; Rev. i. 5. He offered himself a sacrifice to God for sin, and the blood of the slain sacrifice is sprinkled on the sinners in him, for their cleansing: 1 John i. 7, "The blood of Jesus Christ his Son cleanseth us from all sin." The stain of sin was so deep, that nothing else could wash it out: and had he not provided the laver of his own blood, Abraham, Paul, and all the saints now in glory, since they were once filthy, would have been filthy still, with Cain, Judas, and other filthy vessels of wrath.

There are two things in his blood, that make it to wash out this stain, as deep as it is.

1*st*, An infinite value and dignity; for it is the blood of an infinite person, the blood of God, Acts xx. 28, the Son of God, 1 John i. 7, the Father's equal, the Most High.

2*dly*, An infinite efficacy, power, and energy; for the Spirit is in it, the infinite Spirit of holiness, John vi. 53. with 63. The blood was given for atonement, because the life of the flesh, or the animal spirits, are in the blood, Lev. xvii. 11. And therefore it was to be sprinkled while it was yet warm with the spirits in it. Now, Christ's blood is always warm and fresh, with the spirits of life and holiness in it, Heb. x. 20; Rev. iii. 1.

4. There is a twofold washing by the blood of Christ; one that makes clean in the eye of the law, leaving not the least mark of a spot on the soul; peculiar to the saints in heaven, Heb. xii. 23. Another, making clean in the eye of the gospel, though not absolutely: John xv. 3, "Now ye are clean through the word which I have spoken unto you." Cant. iv. 7, "Thou art all fair, my love, there is no spot in thee." It is this last our text means only. Only observe, that they are not different kinds, but different degrees of the same washing by Christ's blood. It is the same laver of Christ's blood, that we are washed in before death to fit us for communion with God here, and that same laver that we are washed in at death, to fit us for communion with God in heaven. Only that efficacy of Christ's blood now exerted on us in part, is put forth on us in full measure to the utter abolition of sin, Eph. v. 25, 26, 27; Rev. vii. 14, 15.

5. As washing is properly the purging away of filthiness, spots, and stains from the object washed; so the washing from sin is formally and directly the sanctification of the sinner, Eph. v. 26; Tit. iii. 5. So if Christ sanctify us not, we have no part in him. Howbeit, it supposes or implies more than that wherein it formally consists.

In all washing there are two things to be distinguished: the loosing of the filth sticking to the object; for if it do not stick, it cannot defile: and the removing of it being once loosed, which is the washing properly. Accordingly in washing a soul from sin, there are two things.

1*st*, The loosing of the filth of sin sticking to the soul. Sin sticks to our souls, as pitch or tar to a man's fingers: and there is no removing of it, till once it be loosed by an application of Christ's blood. Now, it is by guilt that it sticks to our soul, 1 Cor. xv. 56. And that is done away in our justification; which must needs go before our sanctification, as the loosing of sticking filth, before the washing it away; as the Holy Ghost teacheth, Rom. vii. 6, "But now we are delivered from the law, that being dead wherein we were held; that we should serve in newness of spirit, and not in the oldness of the letter." Hence the apostle saith of the Corinthians, 1 Cor. vi. 11, "And such were some of you: but ye are washed, but ye are sanctified, but ye are justified in the name of the Lord Jesus, and by the Spirit of our God."

2*dly*, The removing and purging away the filth of sin, being once loosed: and the same blood that looses it, purgeth it away in sanctification, as the same water that looseth the filth, carries it away off the cloth; and so the pardoned sinner is made holy: Heb. ix. 14, "How much more shall the blood of Christ, who, through the eternal Spirit, offered himself without spot to God, purge your conscience from dead works to serve the living God?" Rev. vii. 14, "These are they which came out of great tribulation, and have washed their robes, and made them white in the blood of the Lamb." And this purging away of the filth of sin off the sinner, lies in three things.

(1.) The putting away of his former loathsomeness before God. The blood of Christ having come over the soul, it is now washed, and God can look on it with complacency, Rev. i. 5, 6. He calls her beloved, that was not beloved.

(2.) Making of the soul fair and clean before the Lord: Cant. iv. 7, "Thou art all fair, my love, there is no spot in thee." The Spirit in the blood leaves his own image on the soul, and carries it all over the man, 2 Cor. iii. 18; Tit. i. 14. Life, eternal life, is in that blood, and wherever it comes; and it goes over the whole man, seeds of life are left in the soul that shall never die out. The Spirit in the blood takes of the fulness of grace in Christ, and communicates to them grace for grace, John i. 16, so transforming them into his image.

(3.) Removing the legal shame out of the soul before God, and causing it, with child-like kindly blushes, to come before him, and press near him, crying, Abba, Father, with the boldness of faith in greater or lesser measure: Rom. viii. 15, "For ye have not received the spirit of bondage again to fear; but ye have received the Spirit of adoption, whereby we cry, Abba, Father." Ezra ix. 6, "O my God, I am ashamed and blush to lift up my face to thee, my God: for our iniquities are increased over our head, and our trespass is grown up unto the heavens."

6. Faith is the instrumental cause of this washing. Hence the apostle, Acts xv. 9, speaks of "purifying the heart by faith." It lays hold upon, and applies the blood of Christ: Rom. iii. 25, "Whom God hath set forth to be a propitiation, through faith in his blood, to declare his righteousness for the remission of sins."

7. *Lastly*, Afflictions are the occasional causes of this washing: Is. xxvii. 9, "By this therefore shall the iniquity of Jacob be purged, and this is all the fruit to take away his sin."

III. The next thing to be considered, is the inseparableness of the two. They are so,

1. In respect of their subject, which is necessarily one. He that has the one, has the other; and no man can have either of them singly. If thou hast part in Christ, thou art washed by him; if thou art washed by him, thou hast part with him.

2. In respect of time. That moment one gets part with Christ, he washes him from his sins. In order of nature indeed, part with Christ goes before washing, and justification before sanctification. But in respect of time they come together and at once. That they are so inseparable, appears,

1*st*, From the end and design of Christ's death, which cannot be frustrated. He died for that end, that sinners taking part with him by faith, might be washed by him from their sins, Eph. v. 25, &c.; Tit. ii. 14.

2*dly*, From the nature of the thing. There is a lively efficacy in Christ's blood to wash away sin: so that the soul come to Christ, and having part in him, must needs be washed; or that precious blood must be counted as dead water, that has lost its virtue, Heb. x. 20. Can a foul garment be laid in a pure running stream, and the washing of it not be begun the moment that it is laid in? And can an unholy soul be united by faith to Christ, and the washing of it not begun that moment by virtue from his blood?

Use I. Of trial. Ye may hereby know whether ye have any part with Christ or not, and consequently whether ye have a right to the Lord's table or not? Are ye washed by Christ from your sins, or not? If ye are unsanctified, unholy souls, yet living in the filth of your sins, I declare ye have no part with Christ; since where there is no true holiness, there is no true faith.

QUESTION. How may I know that I am washed by Christ?

MARK 1. If ye are washed by Christ, though ye are not washed perfectly, ye are washed universally: washed in every part, though not perfectly clean in any part: 2. Cor. v. 17. "If any man be in Christ he is a new creature: old things are past away, behold all things are become new." Ye are washed from the gross pollutions of the outward man, from the reigning pollutions of the inner man: Psal. xxiv 3. 4, "Who shall ascend into the hill of the Lord? and who shall stand in his holy place? He that hath clean hands, and a pure heart; who hath not lift up his soul unto vanity, nor sworn deceitfully." There is a new set in you for purity, darting to all the points of the Christian compass, though you fall short of degrees in every point. That compass ye find, 1 John iii. 3. "And every man that hath this hope in him, purifieth himself, even as he is pure."

2. Ye lay the stress of your acceptance with God, not upon your inherent cleanness, the effect of your washing; but on the blood of Christ, the cause of it: Philip. iii. 3. "For we are the circumcision, which worship God in the spirit, and rejoice in Christ Jesus, and have no confidence in the flesh." Close hypocrites never fail to split on this rock. That, Matth. v. 3. "Blessed are the poor in spirit; for theirs is the kingdom of heaven," is set first, for it must be carried through all;" and ver. 8. "Blessed are the pure in heart; for they shall see God."

3. Your hearts are loosed from sin, though it cleaves to you. It lies not like mud in a pool, where there is nothing to wear it out; but like mud in a spring, where the spring-water tends to work it out. So ye will be groaning under the remains of your uncleanness, saying, with the Apostle, Rom. vii. 24. "O wretched man that I am! who shall deliver me from the body of this death?" You will be content to see every spot, Psal. cxxxix. 23, 24, that it may be washed off; and really desirous to be made perfectly clean; as was the Apostle, Philip. iii. 13, 14, "I count not myself to have apprehended: but this one thing I do, forgetting those things which are behind, and reaching forth unto those things which are before, I press toward the mark, for the prize of the high calling of God in Christ Jesus."

USE 2. Of instruction and direction to unwashed souls yet lying in their blood. Sinners, will ye be made clean?

For MOTIVE: To be left lying in the filth of sin, is formally one half of the punishment of the damned, and virtually the whole of it. See the form of Christ's giving up with a sinner, and dropping him for ever, Rev. xxii. 11. "He that is unjust, let him be unjust still: and he which is filthy, let him be filthy still." There is the punishment of loss. And in that filth will be bred and fed the worm that never dies; out of it will arise the fire that is never quenched. And that is the punishment of sense.

Now, the DIRECTION is, If ye would be washed by Christ, get part with Christ. Say not, Will ever I get part with Christ being so unclean, not purified and meet for him? But no uncleanness of yours can hinder your getting part with Christ, if you will but take it. See the case of the Corinthians, 1. Cor. vi. 11. "And such were some of you: but ye are washed, but ye are sanctified, but ye are justified in the name of the Lord Jesus, and by the Spirit of our God." And ye shall rot and pine away in your filth, wash otherwise as well as ye will, if ye will not take it: Psal. lxxxi. 11, 12, "But my people would not hearken to my voice: and Israel would none of me. So I gave them up unto their own hearts' lust: and they walked in their own counsels."

QUESTION. What access have I to get part with Christ? ANSWER. Christ and his salvation are a common good: 1. John iv. 14. "We have seen, and do testify, that the Father sent the Son to be the Saviour of the world." Jude ver. 3. this salvation is called "the common salvation." I proclaim to every one to come and take their part with Christ, assuring them of welcome: Rev. xxii. 17. "And the Spirit and the bride say, Come. And let him that heareth, say, Come. And let him that is athirst, come: And whosoever will, let him take the water of life freely."

QUESTION. How may I be possessed of part with Christ? ANSWER. By faith, crediting the promise of the gospel, and accordingly trusting on Christ as your Saviour, for his whole salvation; for salvation from sin as well as from wrath; for that holiness and purity of heart and life, which are absolutely necessary to make you meet for the inheritance of the saints in light, as well as for that righteousness by which you can only be accepted in the sight of God, and by which alone you can have a sure and indefeasible title to heaven and glory.

Lastly, Let the saints consider, that the more part they have with Christ, the more they will be washed; and that faith is the only way to have part with Christ in all his saving benefits, and that it is a mean, of God's appointment, for washing and purification. Hence be exercising faith daily upon Christ, and particularly in the view of going to a communion table, in order to your being washed and sanctified; remembering, that unless Christ wash you, you can have no part with him.

THE MYSTERY OF SANCTIFICATION BY CHRIST.

Several sermons preached, at Ettrick, August 25, 1728, and subsequent Lord's days.

John xiii. 8,

If I wash thee not, thou hast no part with me.

I ENTERED on these words last Lord's day, on occasion of the sacramental solemnity which was then celebrated among us; observed a doctrine, proposed a method, which was briefly prosecuted, and I made some practical improvement of the subject. But as this text opens a large field of discourse, and contains ample matter for directing faith and practice, I shall now endeavour to prosecute the design of the words more fully, in a series of discourses. For this end I observe the following doctrine, viz.

DOCTRINE. Such an inseparable connection there is between a sinner's having part with Christ, and being washed from his sins by Christ in a work of sanctification, that if a sinner is not washed from his sins by Christ, he has no part with Christ, while he is so.

Briefly, If a sinner is not washed from his sins by Christ, he has no part with Christ.

In handling this important subject, I shall consider,

I. What it is to be washed from our sins by Christ, viz. unto a cleanness in the eye of the gospel.

II. The unwashed or unsanctified sinner's having no part with Christ.

III. Conclude with some practical inferences.

I. I shall consider what it is to be washed from our sins by Christ, viz. unto a cleanness in the eye of the gospel. And upon this head, I shall shew,
 1. What this washing supposeth.
 2. Wherein it consists.
 3. How it is done and brought about.

First, I shall shew what our being washed from our sins by Christ supposeth.

1. It supposeth in the sinner, a conviction of the filthiness of sin, and his loathsomeness by it. Hence the church says, Is. lxiv. 6, "But we are all as an unclean thing, and all our righteousnesses are as filthy rags, and we all do fade as a leaf, and our iniquities, like the wind, have taken us away." They that never saw the vileness and abominable nature of sin, are not washed from it; Prov. xxx. 12, "There is a generation that are pure in their own eyes, and yet is not washed from their filthiness." The man cries not only, with the criminal, Guilty, guilty; but, with the leper, Unclean, unclean. Sin is not only frightful, but hateful and loathsome to him, as the vilest filth. Now, if ye have not been convinced of the filthiness of sin, ye have no part with Christ.

1*st*, This conviction is got by looking into the glass of the law, representing the spotless holiness of God: Rom. vii. 12, 13, 14, "The law is holy; and the commandment holy, and just, and good. Was then that which is good made death unto me? God forbid. But sin that it might appear sin, working death in me by that which is good; that sin by the commandment might become exceeding sinful. For we know that the law is spiritual: but I am carnal, sold under sin." The glaring beauty of God's holiness expressed in the law, striking the sinner, he sees himself filthy and loathsome before the holy God, as most unlike him.

2*dly*, It fixes an impression of shame on the sinner. He is ashamed of himself, of what he is, what he has done, and what he has neglected to do; as the publican did, Luke xviii. 13. who "standing afar off, would not lift up so much as his eyes unto heaven, but smote upon his breast, saying, God be merciful to me a sinner." He is like a child, that having got a clean white frock on him, has fallen into the mire, and stands ashamed before his mother in that pickle.

2. It supposes a willingness to be made clean: Psal. xix. 12, "Who can understand his errors? cleanse thou me from secret faults." It is not easy to bring a sinner that length: Jer. xiii. 27, "Woe unto thee, O Jerusalem, wilt thou not be made clean? when shall it once be?" Sin is so woven into our nature, and so strength-

ened by custom in sin, which is a second nature, that it is harder to make a sinner willing to be made clean, than to bring a swine away from the mire and dirt it loves to nestle and wallow in. But in the day of the washing of a sinner, he is made as willing to be washed as ever child ashamed of his nastying himself is. So if ye have not been made willing to be clean, ye have no part with Christ.

3. It supposes a conviction that we cannot wash ourselves clean, by any thing we can do or suffer: Rom. vii. 24, "O wretched man that I am! who shall deliver me from the body of this death?" What mars the washing by Christ with many, is, that they think they can wash themselves clean enough by themselves. They see not how fast the filth of sin sticks to them, and so they think their praying, confessing, reforming, and tears, will do it. But hear what Job says, chap. ix. 30, 31, "If I wash myself with snow-water, and make my hand never so clean; yet shalt thou plunge me in the ditch, and mine own clothes shall abhor me." This every soul that is sanctified is brought to. Therefore if ye have not been convinced, that ye cannot wash yourselves clean, by any thing ye can do, ye have no part with Christ.

4. It supposes a hearty consent of the soul to be washed by Christ. Christ washes none against their will: Jer. xiii. 27, "Woe unto thee, O Jerusalem, wilt thou not be made clean? when shall it once be?" They that will needs lie still in their filthiness, shall lie and rot in it for ever for him: Rev. xxii. 11, "He that is unjust, let him be unjust still: and he which is filthy, let him be filthy still." Hos. iv. 17, "Ephraim is joined to idols: let him alone." Christ makes all his elect willing to be holy, but he forces holiness on none. Therefore if ye have not given a hearty consent of your soul to be washed, ye have no part with Christ.

5. *Lastly*, It supposes a presenting of our defiled souls to Christ to be washed by him. This is the work of faith, by which the soul comes to the waters: Is. lv. 1, "Ho, every one that thirsteth, come ye to the waters, and he that hath no money; come ye, buy and eat, yea, come, buy wine and milk without money, and without price." The soul comes to Christ, as the leper to the priest to be cleansed: Psal. li. 7, "Purge me with hyssop, and I shall be clean: wash me, and I shall be whiter than snow." Compared with Lev. xiv. 6, "As for the living bird, he shall take it, and the cedar-wood, and the scarlet, and the hyssop, and shall dip them, and the living bird, in the blood of the bird that was killed over the running water." It eyes him as a Saviour from the filth, as well as the guilt of sin; as a sanctifier of the unclean, as well as a justifier of the ungodly. Therefore, if ye have not presented your

defiled souls to Christ, to be washed by him, ye have no part with Christ.

Secondly, I shall shew wherein our being washed from our sins by Christ consists. As washing in the general consists in removing filthiness, and making clean; so does the washing of a soul by Christ, lie in removing the filth of sin from off the sinner, and making him clean in likeness to God. Now,

1. Christ washeth sinners in the inner man: Psal. xlv. 13, "The King's daughter is all glorious within." Pharisaical washings reach the outer man only: but Christ's washing goes to the hidden man of the heart. Adam left us in the mire of sin, with a nature corrupt and filthy, the very reverse of the nature of God; all the faculties of our souls defiled, Tit. i. 15. But Christ washes our nature and faculties. And this lies in two things.

1*st*, Removing and washing off that filth of sin, that either clave to them from our birth, or has been added to them since: Tit. iii. 5. "Not by works of righteousness, which we have done, but according to his mercy he saved us by the washing of regeneration, and renewing of the Holy Ghost." We came into the world with such corruption cleaving to our nature and faculties, as not only disabled us for all good, but made us prone to all evil, and averse to all good. This is strengthened and increased during the time one lives unregenerate. And the corruption of nature spreads itself, and takes many roots in the soul, in diverse particular lusts, Rom. vi. 12. Now, Christ washing this filth off the soul,

(1.) Purgeth our whole nature and faculties, from that corruption, so far that it does not reign there: Rom. vi. 14, "For sin shall not have dominion over you: for ye are not under the law, but under grace." The total blindness as to the receiving of the things of God, is purged out of the mind; that reigning aversion to good, out of the will; and the reigning carnality, out of the affections. The natural corrupt bent of the heart is taken away, removed, and broken; the stony heart is taken away, and a heart of flesh is given, Ezek. xxxvi. 26.

(2.) He purgeth the soul from its old lusts, loosing them at the root: Gal. v. 24, "They that are Christ's, have crucified the flesh, with the affections and lusts." As in the deluge of waters coming over the earth, trees deeply rooted were washed away by the roots, and lay floating here and there, and so might give some disturbance to the ark: so Christ's efficacious blood coming over the soul, looses old lusts by the roots, though they are not quite taken away, but give disturbance to the believer. They are in him as a broken tooth, they hang at him as a leg out of joint.

2*dly*, It lies in introducing the beauty of habitual holiness into our souls, in conforming us to the image of Christ: Tit. iii. 5, forecited. 2 Cor. iii. 18, "But we all with open face, beholding as in a glass the glory of the Lord, are changed into the same image, from glory to glory, even as by the Spirit of the Lord." As the vessel of brass or silver, being overlaid with nastiness, has nothing of its primitive lustre; yet when it is washed and scoured, it recovers somewhat of its former brightness: so the unwashed sinner has lost all his primitive spiritual glory: but Christ washing him in the day of grace, he recovers it somewhat; and the washing being perfected in glory, he will be brighter and more glorious than ever. Now, Christ introducing this into our soul,

(1.) Implants in us a new nature, which goes over all the faculties of the soul. It is a divine nature, 2 Pet. i. 4, as coming from God, and making the soul like God, John iii. 6, "That which is born of the Spirit, is spirit." Hence the man is a new creature; all his faculties are renewed, mind, will, and conscience: 2 Cor. v. 17, "If any man be in Christ, he is a new creature: old things are past away, behold, all things are become new." This nature has a bent and propensity to good, and an aversion to evil, and cannot lose it as long as it is in being: and it will be ever, for it is an immortal nature. Hence the combat, Gal. v. 17, "The flesh lusteth against the Spirit, and the Spirit against the flesh: and these are contrary the one to the other; so that ye cannot do the things that ye would."

(2.) This new nature hath in it the seeds of all saving graces: 1 John iii. 9, "Whosoever is born of God, doth not commit sin; for his seed remaineth in him: and he cannot sin, because he is born of God." Compared with Deut. xxx. 6, "The Lord thy God will circumcise thine heart, and the heart of thy seed, to love the Lord thy God with all thine heart and with all thy soul, that thou mayest live." We have a swatch of them, Gal. v. 22, 23, "The fruit of the Spirit is love, joy, peace, long-suffering, gentleness, goodness, faith, meekness, temperance." And they are taken out of that fulness of grace that is in Christ the head, and communicated to the sinner as a member: John i. 16. "And of his fulness have all we received, and grace for grace." And thus they bear the image of Christ, that as he was meek, lowly, &c. so are they in a measure. And hereby they are enabled for all acts of holy obedience, as a principle of life gives power for motion.

This is the washing of the sinner in the inner man: and if ye are not so washed by Christ, ye have no part with him.

2. Christ washeth sinners in the outward man too: Psal. xlv. 13.

"The King's daughter is all glorious within; her clothing is of wrought gold." These two go together, the latter issuing from the former: Psal. xxiv. 3. 4. "Who shall ascend into the hill of the Lord? and who shall stand in his holy place? He that hath clean hands and a pure heart; who hath not lift up his soul unto vanity, nor sworn deceitfully." James iv. 8. "Cleanse your hands, ye sinners, and purify your hearts, ye double-minded." As the candle within shines through the lantern, so grace in the heart appears in the outward conversation: Matth. vi. 22. "The light of the body is the eye: if therefore thine eye be single, thy whole body shall be full of light." As the corruption of nature reigning, vents itself in abominable works, Psal. xiv. 1; so the cleansing and purifying of our nature, vents itself in good works, Tit. ii. 14. "Christ gave himself for us, that he might redeem us from all iniquity, and purify unto himself a peculiar people zealous of good works." "For as the tree is, so will the fruit be."

Now, Christ washing sinners in the outward man.

1*st*, Removes the filth that before clave to their life and conversation, Eph. iv. 22. It is no more a vile conversation, nay, nor a vain conversation, 1 Peter i. 18; not a disorderly, but a well-ordered conversation, Psal. l. 23. They that go back to their former conversation, whether in vanity or vileness, shew themselves but Satan's washed swine, not Christ's washed saints, 2. Pet ii. 22. It reaches,

(1.) Their words, and purifies them from corrupt communication.

If the heart be circumcised, so will the lips be too: James i 26. "If any man among you seem to be religious, and bridleth not his tongue, but deceiveth his own heart, this man's religion is vain." If grace rule in the heart, the tongue will not be allowed to go at random. The liberty that some take with their tongues in obscenity, lying, swearing, mocking and jesting at serious religion, &c. proclaims them to be unwashed by Christ. See Psal. xv.

(2.) It reaches the course of their actions, and purifies it: Heb. ix. 14. "How much more shall the blood of Christ, who, through the eternal Spirit, offered himself without spot to God, purge your conscience from dead works to serve the living God?" It purifies their course from impiety against God, and injustice against man; teaching them to walk, as Tit. ii. 12. "Soberly, righteously, and godly." Their hands are washed, as well as their hearts: and their feet are washed, that they go not in the way of sinners as before.

2*dly*, He beautifies them in their life and conversation: Cant. vii. 1. "How beautiful are thy feet with shoes, O prince's daughter? the joints of thy thighs are like jewels, the work of the hands of a cunning workman." Compared with Eph. vi. 15. "And your feet shod with the preparation of the gospel of peace." He makes them "shine as lights in the midst of a crooked and perverse generation;" and helps them to a conversation becoming the gospel. And this also reaches,

(1.) Their words. Their tongue is made their glory whereby they glorify God. Instead of corrupt communication, they produce something for the use of edifying. Being translated from the power of darkness into the kingdom of God's dear Son, they learn the language of it.

(2.) The course of their works. They not only cease to do evil but learn to do well, Is. i. 16. 17. They become "zealous of good works," Tit. ii. 14. As it is but half washing that takes away only the gross filth, but makes not clean: so it is but half Christianity, where people satisfy themselves with not doing evil, but set not themselves to do good.

Thirdly, I shall shew how our being washed from our sins by Christ is done and brought about. Christ washeth sinners, making use of several things to that blessed purpose.

First, Christ washeth sinners, using some things more immediately for that purpose towards them. And,

First, Christ washeth sinners with his blood, as the most immediate cause of their cleansing. Hence the church ascribes praise to Christ, "who loved them and washed them from their sins in his own blood," Rev. i. 5. The blood of Christ hath that place in washing of defiled souls, that water hath in washing defiled bodies: so it is the holy water wherewith we are washed from our sins. Therefore it is called a fountain, and that not only to drink at, but to wash at: Zech. xiii. 1, "In that day there shall be a fountain opened to the house of David, and to the inhabitants of Jerusalem, for sin and for uncleanness." Compared with 1 John i. 7, "The blood of Jesus Christ his Son cleanseth us from all sin." This blood being applied to the soul polluted with sin, it effectually removes the filth of sin from the soul.

For understanding this, these things are to be noted.

1. The defilement or uncleanness sin leaves on the soul, is not a bodily and visible thing, as nastiness on our bodies or clothes, which may be taken away with hands: but it is a moral and spiritual uncleaness, viz., an unlikeness or contrariety to the holiness of God expressed in his law; so that the washing of a soul from it is the rendering of that soul like unto God in his imitable perfections, expressed in the ten commandments, which express his image unto us, that appeared perfectly in the man Christ, being and walking exactly in every point according to these ten commands, in all their spirituality and extent.

2. By the blood of Christ in this matter, is not meant simply the blood that ran out of his veins in his circumcision, the sufferings of his life, and crucifixion; but Christ himself sacrificed for us; which sacrifice was begun from the moment of his incarnation, was continued all his life long, was perfected on the cross and in the grave, and received its actual purifying efficacy in his resurrection, as a sacrifice fully offered, and accepted for the ends it was offered for: Tit. ii. 14, " He gave himself for us, that he might redeem us from all iniquity, and purify unto himself a peculiar people zealous of good works. Rom. iv. 23, " Who was delivered for our offences, and was raised again for our justification." 1 Cor. vi. 11, " And such were some of you: but ye are washed, but ye are sanctified, but ye are justified in the name of the Lord Jesus, and by the Spirit of our God." Hence we owe our sanctification to the holiness of his nature, and the righteousness of his life, as well as to his death; the former being as essentially requisite to make him an effectual sacrifice for us, as the latter; since no sacrifice could atone, but what was without natural and accidental blemish. But his blood is particularly named in the case,

1*st*, For that the life going away with the blood in all living creatures, and so in the man Christ, the shedding of his blood was the perfecting stroke in his sacrificing himself for us: so that we are said to be washed with his blood, as the prisoner is said to be delivered by his cautioner's paying the utmost farthing of his debt. See Rom. i. 17, " For therein is the righteousness of God revealed from faith to faith: as it is written, The just shall live by faith." Compared with Rom. iii. 25, " Whom God hath set forth to be a propitiation, through faith in his blood, to declare his righteousness for the remission of sins."

2*dly*, For decency of expression, the term blood being most agreeable to the term washing, which relates to some liquid. Agreeable hereto was it, that after Christ being born holy, had lived holy, and died on the cross, his side was pierced, and there came forth blood and water fitted to wash: the Holy Ghost thereby teaching, that the washing or sanctifying of sinners was to proceed from Christ, in his holy birth, life, and death; thence was the spring of purifying virtue from sin.

3. As it is by applying water to the unclean thing, that it is washed: so it is by applying to our souls, Christ sacrificed for us, that we are sanctified and washed from sin. A man may stand at a river side bedaubed with mire and dirt, till he die; and yet be never a whit the cleaner if the water of that river, be not brought close upon him: so Christ, in the purifying virtue of his blood, may

be within reach of the sinner's hand all his days, and yet he may die in his filth of sin, and lie in it in hell for ever, if Christ and he never come close together in a spiritual union. The blood of sacrifices was first offered to God for atonement, and then it was sprinkled on persons or things for their purification: Heb. ix. 19, "For when Moses had spoken every precept to all the people according to the law, he took the blood of calves and of goats, with water, and scarlet wool, and hyssop, and sprinkled both the book and all the people." Compared with Exod. xxiv. 5—8, "And Moses sent young men of the children of Israel, which offered burnt-offerings, and sacrificed peace-offerings of oxen unto the Lord. And Moses took half of the blood, and put it in basons; and half of the blood he sprinkled on the altar. And he took the book of the covenant, and read in the audience of the people: and they said, All that the Lord hath said, will we do, and be obedient. And Moses took the blood, and sprinkled it on the people, and said, Behold the blood of the covenant, which the Lord hath made with you concerning all these words." The offering of the blood of Christ to God is over, near seventeen hundred years ago: but the sprinkling or application of it is still going on: Heb. xii. 22, 24, "But ye are come—to Jesus the Mediator of the new covenant, and to the blood of sprinkling, that speaketh better things than that of Abel." Where it is sprinkled, they are cleansed; where not, they lie still in their filth, having no more cleansing from sin by it, than if it had never been shed.

4. It is not every water that will wash clean; but there is a cleansing virtue in some water, that is not in other water. I am not to inquire into the cause of that difference; but into the cause of the cleansing virtue of the blood of Christ, whereby we are washed from sin, that is not in any other thing, though men have multiplied things for that end. If we inquire into the spring of the cleansing virtue that is in Christ sacrificed for us, and in no other things, we find these two.

1*st*, There is a real and proper merit of sinners' sanctification in him. By his sacrifice of himself he has merited at the hand of God the sanctification of us, and washing us from our sin: Eph. v. 25, 26, "Christ loved the church, and gave himself for it: that he might sanctify and cleanse it with the washing of water by the word." Christ as really merited our personal holiness, and every good work we do, at the hand of God, as he merited the pardon of atheism and blasphemy to us: so absurd is the merit of our works: Tit. ii. 14, "He gave himself for us, that he might redeem us from all iniquity, and purify unto himself a peculiar people, zealous of good works." 1 Pet. i. 18, 19, "Ye know that ye were not redeemed with corruptible things, as silver and gold, from your vain conversation received by tradition from your fathers; but with the precious blood of Christ, as of a lamb without blemish and without spot." Now, there is no such merit in any thing else, that they should wash.

Hence Christ being applied to the soul, or his blood sprinkled on it, has a loosing efficacy, that the filth of sin is loosed from the soul it stuck close to before: even as the payment of the ransom applied to the captive, actually looses the bond of his captivity; so as a just judge can no more suffer him to be a captive, a prisoner. I shewed before, that it is guilt that is that bond. Wherefore, for persons to pretend part with Christ, while yet their filth of sin sticks as close to them, and they to it, as ever, is to blaspheme the justice of the Father, or the merit of the Son; as if either the one did receive the ransom, and yet not set the captive free; or else the other's merit was defective, and therefore ineffectual.

2*dly*, There is a fulness of the Spirit of holiness in him, or in his blood. Hence he is said, Rev. iii. 1, to have "the seven Spirits of God." Christ sacrificed for us, is the receptacle of the Spirit of sanctification, as the animal spirits are in the blood while fresh and warm, as Christ's blood always is: that is, Christ himself as sacrificed, Heb. x. 20. And that Spirit of sanctification is not in other things, not in Popish penances, not in the legal performances of prayers, tears, confessions, resolutions, &c. which many Protestants use for washing themselves. All these in this case are but dead water, congealed blood without spirits, that defile, but cannot wash.

Hence Christ being applied to, or his blood sprinkled on a soul, has a cleansing efficacy, removing the filth of sin, and cleansing and brightening the soul in likeness to God: 2 Cor. iii. 18, "But we all with open face, beholding as in a glass the glory of the Lord, are changed into the same image, from glory to glory, even as by the Spirit of the Lord." Thus Christ speaking of that application of himself to sinners, as by eating and drinking, which are most close even to the incorporating the meat and drink with the feeder, John vi. 53, 54, "Then Jesus said unto the Jews, Verily verily I say unto you, Except ye eat the flesh of the Son of man, and drink his blood, ye have no life in you. Whoso eateth my flesh, and drinketh my blood, hath eternal life, and I will raise him up at the last day;" gives this as the reason of the efficacy, ver. 63, "It is the spirit that quickeneth, the flesh profiteth nothing: the words that I speak unto you, they are spirit, and they are life." As filthy sores are washed and cleansed with spirituous liquors, filthy souls are washed and cleansed with the blood of Christ, full of the Spirit of holiness.

Wherefore to pretend to part with Christ, and yet still to live in your sins, without repentance, or reformation and amendment, is to blaspheme either the blood of Christ, or his Spirit; as if either there were no Spirit of holiness in his blood, or else that that Spirit of holiness hath no efficacy to purge away the filth of sin, and make holy.

5. Washing off of filth and making clean, is according to the degree of the application of the water with its cleansing virtue. It is a very slight spot that will be quite washed off at the very first brush. There is virtue enough in the river, at once to wash clean a filthy object; but the washer applies it but by degrees, so that it may be long ere it be got perfectly clean: so there is virtue enough in Christ to wash all whom he washes at all, perfectly clean at once; but that virtue is applied but by degrees, 2 Cor. iii. 18, forecited. Prov. iv. 18, "The path of the just is as a shining light, that shineth more and more unto the perfect day."

There is a threefold washing of sinners, according to a threefold application of Christ's blood to them.

1*st*, A begun washing by a begun application thereof. This is done in the work of conversion. Tit. iii. 5, it is called the washing of regeneration. Here the soul that before all along was lying in wickedness together with the unclean world, being taken out from among them by effectual calling, and united to Christ by faith, and so having part with him, is washed from his filthiness, by an application of the blood of Christ, that never touched him before, but now streams over him in union with Christ: Ezek. xvi. 8, 9, "Now when I passed by thee, and looked upon thee, behold, thy time was the time of love, and I spread my skirt over thee, and covered thy nakedness: yea, I sware unto thee, and entered into a covenant with thee, saith the Lord God, and thou becamest mine. Then washed I thee with water; yea, I throughly washed away thy blood from thee, and I anointed thee with oil."

Concerning the washing, the effect of this application, observe,

(1.) It is a washing all over; a washing of every part, though not quite clean in any part: 2 Cor. v, 17, "If any man be in Christ, he is a new creature: old things are past away, behold, all things are become new." Therefore it is called a new birth: Tit. iii. 5, "Not by works of righteousness, which we have done, but according to his mercy he saved us, by the washing of regeneration, and renewing of the Holy Ghost." John iii. 5, "Except a man be born of water and of the Spirit, he cannot enter into the kingdom of God." We do not say a child is born, when his head, or feet, or an arm are born; but when the whole child is brought forth. Some shew a head, that, with notions of the principles of religion in it, and a tongue to talk of them, seems to be washed; others shew feet, that, by going in the road of outward reformation, and some external duties, seem to be washed. But it is not the washing of regeneration; for it goes not all over them: they are new in some things, but they are just what they were in other things. Trace them to their walk in their employments and relations, to the entertainment given to the beloved lust, to the inner man, and set of their heart with respect to the purity of the holy law; and they are just the same with the world lying in wickedness. That is an evidence, that their washing is with their own nitre and soap, not with the blood of Christ.

(2.) It is a washing that puts one in a state of cleanness, bringing him out of a state of filthiness: John xiii. 10, "He that is washed needeth not, save to wash his feet, but is clean every whit." There is a difference between one lying in a mire, and another that has defiled his feet; though both need washing, the latter needs but to wash his feet. Such is the case of the unregenerate and regenerate: Cant. vi. 10, "Who is she that looketh forth as the morning, fair as the moon, clear as the sun, and terrible as an army with banners?" When the dawning is come, it is true it is not broad day-light; but yet it is day, not night. The moon has her spots, yet she is not filthy, but fair.

(3.) That state of cleanness can never be lost, John xiii. 10, fore-cited. Many seem to be brought to a state of cleanness, but at length they turn apostates: that says, they were never out of the state of filthiness, and the church of God was but beguiled with them, when they took them for persons in a state of cleanness. They that are once washed, will never apostatize, nor go back again to wallow in the mire: 1 John ii. 19, "They went out from us, but they were not of us: for if they had been of us, they would no doubt have continued with us: but they went out, that they might be made manifest, that they were not all of us."

2*dly,* A continued and progressive washing, by a continued progressive application of Christ's blood to the soul. This is done and carried on all along from the first conversion of a sinner, until his death. Therefore though the elders were about the throne in white, yet there was a sea of glass before it, Rev. iv. 4, 6. And the fountain stands opened for the house of David, as well as for the inhabitants of Jerusalem, Zech. xiii. 1; for saints as well as for sinners. They that, deeming themselves once washed, find no need of washing more, proclaim themselves not washed by Christ, as do they who betake themselves for it to another laver. They that are come to Christ for washing, are still coming, 1 Pet. ii. 4.

Two things make this continued washing necessary.

(1.) Continued imperfection in the washing of the soul during this life, Philip. iii. 12. Believers are in no moment of time perfectly clean; in their most shining moments they are still but as the moon, not without their spots. So that they never want matter of exercise, in purging that they may arrive at a perfect purity: 1 John iii. 3, "Every man that hath this hope in him, purifieth himself, even as he is pure."

(2.) New defilements contracted continually. Though they never lose the state of cleanness, yet they are always needing to wash their feet: John xiii. 10, "He that is washed, needeth not, save to wash his feet, but is clean every whit." An allusion to the priests in the temple service. They are all priests to God, and so washed: but while they go about, such is the defiled world they walk in, the remains of defilement in them, that in every thing they contract some spot: James iii. 2, "For in many things we offend all." Their heart and life have so many remaining seeds of corruption, that they never want occasion to pluck up weeds.

Now, this continued washing is by the continued application of Christ's blood, and no other way: 1. John i. 7, "The blood of Jesus Christ his Son cleanseth us from all sin." For,

[1.] This is the way the saints have looked for it; as David, Psal. li. 2. "Wash me throughly from mine iniquity, and cleanse me from my sin." Ver. 7, "Purge me with hyssop, and I shall be clean: wash me, and I shall be whiter than snow." As the lepers could, by no art of their own, be so purified as to be admitted to society, but by the priests sprinkling them; so sinners, by no art or endeavours of their own, can be purified so as to be admitted to fellowship with God, but by the sprinkling of the blood of Christ upon them. Therefore the sea of glass, which is the blood of Christ, stands before the throne, that whosoever would have communion with God, may wash there, and so be fitted for it.

[2.] There is no merit of holiness, nor fulness of the Spirit in any thing else. The doings and sufferings of saints are as free of merit, as those of sinners: Luke xvii. 10, "So likewise ye, when ye shall have done all those things which are commanded you, say, We are unprofitable servants: we have done that which was our duty to do." Neither is there any thing of the Spirit in them, but so far as the blood of Christ is sprinkled on them, rendering them acceptable, Rev. vii. 14; 2 Cor. ii. 16. But in the blood of Christ there is a never-failing merit, a constant fulness of the Spirit, to which the soul may have continual recourse for washing, as to a fountain never dry.

3*dly*, A perfect washing, by a full application of the blood of

Christ. And this takes place at death, Heb. xii. 23—"To the spirits of just men, made perfect." Then believers washed in conversion, and who have been all along washed in the blood of Christ, are by the same means made quite clean and without spot: Eph. v. 25, 26, 27, "Christ loved the church, and gave himself for it: that he might sanctify and cleanse it with the washing of water by the word, that he might present it to himself a glorious church not having spot or wrinkle, or any such thing, but that it should be holy, and without blemish." This lies in two things.

(1.) The doing away the remains of sin wholly. The reigning power of sin being broken by the first application, it is gradually removed by further application, and quite carried off by the full application at death. Not the least stain, nor mark of it, will then be left on the believing soul. But the filth of sin now carried off in part from the whole man, will then be wholly carried off from every part.

(2.) The perfecting of the image of God: 1 John iii, 2, "Beloved, now are we the sons of God, and it doth not yet appear what we shall be: but we know, that when he shall appear, we shall be like him; for we shall see him as he is." The several lineaments of it are indeed drawn now upon the believer, but mixed with corruption in every part: but then it shall be without mixture, every part getting the finishing stroke in that image, 1 Cor. xiii. 10. "But when that which is perfect is come, then that which is in part shall be done away." So shall they "shine as the brightness of the firmament, and as the stars for ever and ever," Dan. xii. 3. "The righteous shall shine forth as the sun, in the kingdom of their Father," Matth. xiii. 43.

Now, it is by a full application of the blood of Christ, that is, by a full participation of Christ crucified in his purifying virtue, that this washing is made: Rev. vii. 14, 15, "These are they which came out of great tribulation, and have washed their robes, and made them white in the blood of the Lamb." Therefore are they before the throne of God, and serve him day and night in his temple: and he that sitteth on the throne shall dwell among them." The cleansing virtue going out from him to the soul in some measure now, will then go out in full measure, as when a sluice is opened, and carries all away before it: 2 Cor. iii. 18, "But we all with open face, beholding as in a glass the glory of the Lord, are changed into the same image, from glory to glory, even as by the Spirit of the Lord." Compared with 1 John iii. 2, forecited. The soul putting off the body, unites more closely with Christ than ever, and so partakes of his merit, and fulness of Spirit, to a pitch of perfection: Eph. iv. 13, "Till we all come in the unity of the faith, and of the knowledge of the Son of God, unto a perfect man, unto the measure of the stature of the fulness of Christ."

Secondly, Christ washeth sinners by his Spirit: Tit. iii. 5, "Not by works of righteousness, which we have done, but according to his mercy he saved us, by the washing of regeneration, and renewing of the Holy Ghost." 2 Thess. ii. 13, "God hath from the beginning chosen you to salvation, through sanctification of the Spirit, and belief of the truth." And the Spirit of Christ has that place in washing defiled souls, that the hand of the washer hath in washing the defiled body of another. The hand being the instrument of action with men, the Spirit of Christ is held forth under that notion, the whole work of the application of Christ's redemption to us being done by him: Acts xi. 21, "And the hand of the Lord was with them: and a great number believed, and turned unto the Lord." Is. liii. 1, "Who hath believed our report? and to whom is the arm of the Lord revealed?" Matt. xii. 28, "But if I cast out devils by the Spirit of God, then the kingdom of God is come unto you." Compared with Luke xi. 20, "But if I with the finger of God cast out devils, no doubt the kingdom of God is come upon you." So Christ washeth sinners with his blood, by his Spirit: John iii. 5, "Except a man be born of water, and of the Spirit, he cannot enter into the kingdom of God." 1 John v. 8, "And there are three that bear witness in earth, the spirit, and the water, and the blood: and these three agree in one." This the apostle very plainly teacheth, 1 Cor. vi. 11, "And such were some of you: but ye are washed, but ye are sanctified, but ye are justified in the name of the Lord Jesus, and by the Spirit of our God." So Christ's hand has never come on that soul for washing, which is destitute of the Spirit of Christ: Rom. viii. 9, "If any man have not the Spirit of Christ, he is none of his."

Now, of the work of the Spirit of Christ in the washing of a sinner, we may take a view in the following particulars.

1. The Spirit of Christ discovers to the sinner his pollution and defilement of soul: John xvi. 8, "And when he is come, he will reprove the world of sin, and of righteousness, and of judgment." He brightens the glass of the holy commandments of the word, and he opens the sinner's eyes, and determines him to look into that glass: and so the sinner, getting a new sight of the holiness and purity of God, Hab. i. 13, gets a new sight of himself, that he cries out, with the leper, Unclean, unclean; and says, with the church, Is. lxiv. 6, "We are all as an unclean thing, and all our righteous-

nesses are as filthy rags." Then he sees that loathsomeness in sin that he saw not before; the loathsomeness of his nature, heart, and life; not excepting those sins he looked on formerly as beauty-spots, glorying in them, Phil. iii. 19. And he is filled with shame and confusion before the Lord; like those, Jer. iii. 22, "Behold, we come unto thee, for thou art the Lord our God." Ver. 25, "We lie down in our shame, and our confusion covereth us: for we have sinned against the Lord our God, we and our fathers from our youth even unto this day, and have not obeyed the voice of the Lord our God." And if ye have no experience of this, ye have no part with Christ.

2. He discovers to the sinner the laver wherein he may be washed from that spiritual pollution, the fountain wherein he may be purified, viz. the blood of Christ, or Christ himself as crucified and sacrificed for us: 1 Cor. ii. 12, "Now we have received, not the spirit of the world, but the Spirit which is of God; that we might know the things that are freely given to us of God." Here is the only effectual mean for purification, the only true purgatory, Jesus Christ in the purifying virtue of his blood, Heb. i. 3. And the Spirit points it out to the sinner. This is called "revealing of the Son," Gal. i. 16; in our Catechism, "enlightening our minds in the knowledge of Christ." Concerning which ye may note,

1*st*, That it is natural to men under a sense of their filthiness, to look to and run to lavers of their own for washing themselves, however ineffectual they are: Hos. v. 13, "When Ephraim saw his sickness, and Judah saw his wound, then went Ephraim to the Assyrian, and sent to king Jareb: yet could he not heal you, nor cure you of your wound." Hence the first question, "What shall we do to be saved?" They have neither eyes to see, nor hearts for the blood of Christ, as the alone mean of washing from sin. The whole ceremonial law pointed the Israelites to Christ as the only remedy for soul pollution, yet they are as great strangers to it, as if they had never heard of it. Hence we have these questions, with the Lord's answer, Mic. vi. 6, 7, 8, "Wherewith shall I come before the Lord, and bow myself before the high God? shall I come before him with burnt-offerings, with calves of a year old? will the Lord be pleased with thousands of rams, or with ten thousands of rivers of oil? shall I give my first-born for my transgression, the fruit of my body for the sin of my soul? He hath shewed thee, O man, what is good; and what doth the Lord require of thee, but to do justly, and to love mercy, and to walk humbly with thy God?"

2*dly* It is the work of the Spirit alone to discover it, so as to bring the unclean soul to it. As Hagar saw not the well though it was near her, till the Lord opened her eyes; so the sinner sees not the opened fountain for sin and uncleanness, till the Spirit enlighten the mind: John xvi. 14, "He shall glorify me: for he shall receive of mine, and shall shew it unto you." And he shews it effectually to the sinner, together with the ineffectualness of all things else for that purpose. And,

(1.) The Spirit shews the ineffectualness of all other, in the glass of the law in its spirituality and extent. There the sinner beholds all that he can do or suffer needs itself to be washed, being polluted and defiled, and so that it can defile him, but not wash him. Hence says the church, Is. lxiv. 6, "But we are all as an unclean thing, and all our righteousnesses are as filthy rags, and we all do fade as a leaf, and our iniquities, like the wind, have taken us away."

(2.) In the glass of the promise of the gospel, he shews the true laver, Christ Jesus: John iii. 16, "For God so loved the world, that he gave his only begotten Son, that whosoever believeth in him, should not perish, but have everlasting life." The Spirit brings home the promise of the gospel, and demonstrates it to the sinner, 1 Cor. ii. 4. And he demonstrates,

[1.] The infallible efficacy of it to cleanse from sin: 1 Thess. i. 5, "For our gospel came not unto you in word only, but also in power, and in the Holy Ghost, and in much assurance." Notwithstanding all that the word saith of the efficacy of Christ's blood to wash from sin, that mystery is but folly to carnal men, till the demonstration of the Spirit come: 1 Cor. i. 23, 24, "But we preach Christ crucified, unto the Jews a stumbling-block, and unto the Greeks foolishness; but unto them which are called, both Jews and Greeks, Christ the power of God, and the wisdom of God." Then the soul says, as Matt. ix. 21, "If I may but touch his garment, I shall be whole."

[2.] The sinner's access to it in particular; that the fountain is not only open, but open for him, 1 Cor. ii. 4, 5. If this be not, the sinner can never apply it to himself by faith. And this the Spirit doth by opening the general warrant of the word, and applying it particularly to the sinner.

3. He brings the sinner into the laver, puts him into the water as it were. We are naturally in the case of that man at the pool, who said, John v. 7, "I have no man, when the water is troubled, to put me into the pool." Though the laver of Christ's blood be near by us, we cannot put in ourselves for washing. Now, the Spirit does the sinner this good office: and he does it by uniting him to Christ, whereby the unclean soul is plunged into the fountain opened

for sin: 1 Cor. xii. 13, "For by one Spirit are we all baptized into one body; and have been all made to drink into one Spirit." And the Spirit brings the sinner into the laver.

1*st*, Passively, entering into the dead and defiled soul whereby the soul is quickened: Ezek. xxxvi. 27, "And I will put my spirit within you, and cause you to walk in my statutes, and ye shall keep my judgments, and do them." Rom. viii. 9, "But ye are not in the flesh, but in the Spirit, if so be that the Spirit of God dwell in you. Now if any man have not the Spirit of Christ, he is none of his." Christ communicates the Spirit, which is his own Spirit dwelling in him, to the dead and defiled soul; and so the soul is passively united to Christ, and quickened. Thus Christ draws the sinner to him for washing, by the Spirit.

2*dly*, Actively, working faith in the sinner, whereby he comes to Christ, and unites with him: Col. ii. 12, "Buried with him in baptism, wherein also you are risen with him through the faith of the operation of God, who hath raised him from the dead." Compared with 2 Cor. iv. 13, "We having the same spirit of faith, according as it is written, I believed, and therefore have I spoken: we also believe, and therefore speak." Eph. iii. 17, "That Christ may dwell in your hearts by faith." The soul being drawn, runs; being united to Christ, unites with him; being put into the opened fountain, dips himself over head and ears in it, Rom. iii. 25. This actual believing the Spirit produces in the sinner immediately out of the spiritual life given by the communication of himself to him: Philip ii. 13, "For it is God which worketh in you, both to will and to do of his good pleasure." John v. 25, "Verily, verily, I say unto you, the hour is coming, and now is, when the dead shall hear the voice of the Son of God: and they that hear shall live." Compared with chap. i. 12, 13, "But as many as received him, to them gave he power to become the sons of God, even to them that believe on his name: which were born, not of blood, nor of the will of the flesh, nor of the will of man, but of God."

Now, the unclean sinner thus brought to Christ, and united to him, is in the fountain, and cannot miss to be washed from his sins with the blood of Christ: and the only hand that brings him there is the Spirit of Christ. Now, he has part with Christ, communion necessarily following upon the union.

4. *Lastly*, The Spirit washeth the unclean soul in the laver, applying Christ to it in the purifying virtue of his blood; as one washeth an unclean person in water, applying the water to him; 1 Pet. i. 2, "Elect according to the foreknowledge of God the Father, through sanctification of the Spirit unto obedience, and sprink-

ling of the blood of Jesus Christ." And according to the degree of that application of Christ to the sinner, in the purifying virtue of his blood, made by the Spirit, such is the degree of the sanctification or washing of the sinner. For understanding this mystery, consider,

1*st*, The soul being united to Christ, is clothed with his merit, as for justification, so for sanctification also: Rev. iii. 18, " I counsel thee to buy of me white raiment, that thou mayest be clothed, and that the shame of thy nakedness do not appear." Sanctification is a great privilege and costly, bought with the Redeemer's blood : 1 Pet. i. 18, 19, " Ye know that ye were not redeemed with corruptible things, as silver and gold, from your vain conversation received by tradition from your fathers ; but with the precious blood of Christ, as of a lamb without blemish and without spot." Tit. ii. 14, " Who gave himself for us, that he might redeem us from all iniquity, and purify unto himself a peculiar people, zealous of good works." And the merit or righteousness of Christ being on a man, by union with Christ, is the ground in law for his partaking of the benefit of sanctification, as a benefit purchased for him : even as the guilt of Adam's first sin on us, is the ground in law for God's denying us the sanctification of our nature in our birth, upon which the corruption of nature is conveyed to us from Adam.

2*dly*, Sinners united to Jesus Christ, have communion with him in his death and resurrection ; *i. e.*, they have a common interest with him therein, they are in law reckoning their death and resurrection too : Col. ii. 12, " Buried with him in baptism, wherein also you are risen with him through the faith of the operation of God, who hath raised him from the dead." The reason is, because Christ died and rose again as a public person, their head, in their name : Rom. vi. 4, " Therefore we are buried with him by baptism into death ; that like as Christ was raised up from the dead by the glory of the Father, even so we also should walk in newness of life." And this communion with Christ in his death and resurrection, is the spring of their sanctification ; it is that which sets all the wheels in motion, that concur to the washing them from their sins : Rom. vi. 3—6, " Know ye not, that so many of us as were baptized into Jesus Christ, were baptized into his death ? Therefore we are buried with him by baptism into death : that like as Christ was raised up from the dead by the glory of the Father, even so we also should walk in newness of life. For if we have been planted together in the likeness of his death : we shall be also in the likeness of his resurrection : knowing this, that our old man is crucified with him, that the body of sin might be destroyed, that henceforth we should not serve sin."

3*dly*, Christ dying put off from himself the whole body of all our sins, which before were upon him by imputation; and rose again without sin imputed, as he was ever without sin inherent: Rom. vi. 10, "For in that he died, he died unto sin once: but in that he liveth, he liveth unto God." For he by his death having fully satisfied for sins, the guilt of them whereby they clave to him, was dissolved of course, and he shook them all off as Paul did the viper into the fire, having no more power to cleave to him or hurt him. Which death and resurrection being of a public person, their head, hath, by the merit thereof, a power of conforming all his members thereto, in dying to sin, and rising to newness of life; even as there was a contrary power in Adam's sin and death: Philip. iii. 10, "That I may know him, and the power of his resurrection, and the fellowship of his sufferings, being made conformable unto his death." Compared with Rom. vi. 5, 6, above-cited.

4*thly*, Sinners having communion with Christ in this his death and resurrection, are in him legally dead to sin, freed from it in point of right, and alive spiritually to God: Rom. vi. 10, 11, "For in that he died, he died unto sin once: but in that he liveth, he liveth unto God. Likewise reckon ye also yourselves to be dead indeed unto sin; but alive unto God through Jesus Christ our Lord." The body of the sins of the flesh is legally put off them, and they are clean: even as the captive or prisoner to whom is legally applied the paying of the ransom or debt by the cautioner, is, in the moment of that application, legally free, and no more a captive or prisoner in point of right; though it may take some time ere he be brought freely out of the dungeon, and his prison garments be got all of them off, and his irons be all knocked off.

5*thly*, Upon this ground the Spirit applies Christ's death and resurrection really to them, conforming them in their own persons thereto: even as when the judge hath legally applied the payment of the ransom to the captive, by sustaining it as paid for him; a messenger applies it really by opening the prison-doors, knocking off the chains, and bringing him out: Gal. vi. 14, "But God forbid that I should glory, save in the cross of our Lord Jesus Christ, by whom the world is crucified unto me, and I unto the world." Philip. iii. 10, "That I may know him, and the power of his resurrection, and the fellowship of his sufferings, being made conformable unto his death." Compared with 1 Pet. i. 2, "Elect according to the foreknowledge of God the Father, through sanctification of the Spirit unto obedience, and sprinkling of the blood of Jesus Christ." So that by the Spirit they are changed into the image of Christ dead and risen again: 2 Cor. iii. 18, "But we all with open face, beholding as in a glass the glory of the Lord, are changed into the same image, from glory to glory, even as by the Spirit of the Lord," Rom. vi. 5, "For if we have been planted together in the likeness of his death; we shall be also in the likeness of his resurrection."

6thly, The Spirit applies Christ's blood, death, and resurrection, to sinners, really, by conveying from Christ the head, unto them as his members, a certain measure and degree of that all-fulness of grace that is lodged in him, which he did to purchase, and rose again to apply: Col. i. 19, "For it pleased the Father, that in him should all fulness dwell, John i. 16, "And of his fulness have all we received, and grace for grace." Compared with John xvi. 14, 15, "He shall glorify me: for he shall receive of mine, and shall shew it unto you. All things that the Father hath, are mine: therefore said I, that he shall take of mine, and shall shew it unto you." All the grace that is in the saints in heaven or earth, or ever shall be, comes from the fulness of grace in the man Christ; as all the light of the world from the sun: and the Spirit communicates it to them from him. Now, all graces are in Christ, and the Spirit communicates to his members of them all, John i. 16, forecited.

7thly, Thus the blood of Christ applied by the Spirit, penetrates or seeks in to the unclean soul, to the washing it from its filthiness; Ezek. xxxvi. 25, "I will sprinkle clean water upon you, and ye shall be clean: from all your filthiness, and from all your idols will I cleanse you." For wherever that grace comes, it must needs have a twofold effect: (1.) To remove sin according to its measure, and so to carry off spiritual filthiness. Where humility comes, pride goes; where heavenliness of mind takes place, there sensuality and worldliness are dislodged; and so of other graces. For grace and sin are two contraries; whereof as the one gains, the other must needs lose. (2.) To beautify and brighten the soul. Hence she is, like "the king's daughter, all glorious within; her clothing is of wrought gold," Psal. xlv. 13. For the more grace one has, the more he is like God. And this grace is immediately derived to us from Christ; who is the image of the invisible God, and therefore fairer than the children of men, Psal. xlv. 2; that we being thereby rendered like Christ, may be rendered like God, in his imitable perfections.

8thly, This communication of grace, by the Spirit, from Christ, to us being united to Christ, is the Spirit's applying Christ's blood to us; inasmuch as the blood of Christ is as it were the vehicle of his grace, as the water is of the soap, that cleansing thing, Mal. iii. 2, Christ is like fuller's soap. In this view is that prayer for sanctification, Psal. li. 2, "Wash me throughly from mine iniquity, and cleanse me from my sin." Wash me, namely, as a fuller doth. In vain is the soap used without the water for washing; and in vain will we look for sanctification by the grace of Christ, without the merit of his blood on us. It is in the stream of his blood going over our souls, that his grace is brought into and left in them, to the beautifying of them in holiness. By the merit of it, it hath a double effect. One relative, and immediate, to our justification. Hence the apostle, Heb. xii. 24, speaks of "coming to Jesus the Mediator of the new covenant, and to the blood of sprinkling, that speaketh better things than that of Abel." Another effect it has, real, and mediate, to our sanctification. Hence the apostle describes Christians as, 1 Pet. i. 2, "Elect according to the foreknowledge of God the Father, through sanctification of the Spirit unto obedience, and sprinkling of the blood of Jesus Christ." And this is effected through the grace of Christ that it brings down with it. It is the bruising of the bread-corn that fits it to be bread; the dying of the corn of wheat, that brings forth more wheat: so it is the crucifying of Christ, that fitted him to be a fountain of grace, whereof sinners might drink; it is the blood or death of Christ that makes Christians, *i. e.* men after his image, John xii. 24. Thus the Spirit's conveying of grace from Christ to us, is his sprinkling us with the blood of Christ for our sanctification, 1 Pet. i. 2; to be distinguished, though not divided, from the sprinkling for our justification, Heb. xii. 24.

Lastly, According to the measure of the former sprinkling or application of the blood of Christ, so is the measure of our sanctification, purification, and cleansing from sin. The other having only a relative and immediate effect, is not capable of degrees: so it is alike in all believers. But this having a real and mediate effect through the grace conveyed in it, is made in very different degrees and measures, as a spring or fountain running into a vessel. And there are three degrees of this application of Christ's blood by the Spirit, as before observed.

1*st,* A begun application of it, in the soul's union with Christ at first in effectual calling. That moment the sinner becomes a member of Christ, the Spirit begins the application of Christ's blood to him for his sanctification, conveying real inherent grace to him from Christ his head, 2 Thess. ii. 13, compared with John xvi. 14, and i. 16. The sluice of grace in Christ that was quite stopt before as to the sinner, is then opened in a measure to run over him for his washing from sin. And as to this measure,

1. It is some measure of all saving grace that is then communicated to the believer from Christ, his head, by the Spirit: John i. 16, "And of his fulness have all we received, and grace for grace."

As the wax receives every point in the seal, so the believer receives every grace in the man Christ. Hence the apostle, Eph. i. 13, speaks of believers being "sealed with the Holy Spirit of promise. As all saving graces are lodged in Christ without measure, John. iii. 34, so a seed of them all is communicated to his members, 1 John iii. 9, of faith, love, repentance, or a set of heart turning God-ward, humility, meekness, &c. And though some graces may be more apparent and topping in a believer, than others; yet he wants none of them altogether, Heb. viii. 10. The effect of this is the habitual sanctification of the believer, whereby the dominion of sin is broken; the pollution and defilement by sin is begun to be removed, and the soul is made habitually holy. More particularly, hereby,

1*st*, The believer's nature is renewed, Eph. iv. 23, 24. He is renewed in the whole man, his whole person, soul and body, 1 Thess. v. 23. There are quite new qualities derived from Christ, into his mind, will, and affections; habits of grace infused into them by the Spirit from Christ, which habits of grace are the immediate principle of gracious actings, distinct from the new vital powers that go before faith. The body is renewed in communion with the renewed soul. Hence the apostle exhorts the Romans, Rom. vi. 13, "Neither yield ye your members as instruments of unrighteousness unto sin: but yield yourselves unto God, as those that are alive from the dead; and your members as instruments of righteousness unto God." So sanctification is quite another thing than the bare amending of our lives; and holiness quite another thing than moral virtue, which can never give us this new nature.

2*dly*, He becomes a new creature, 2 Cor. v. 17; not only a spiritually living creature, as in the quickening of the dead soul, John v. 25, before faith in effectual calling, called the first regeneration, John i. 12, 13, answering to the conception in natural generation; but a new creature in all its parts, by the work of sanctification; a second regeneration, following after faith, and answering to the forming of the conception into the distinct members in the womb, however small, Tit. iii. 5; Eph. ii. 10; i. 13. Hence there is not only a new head, feet, or life, in the case; but a new man, where all saving graces concur, as all the several members in a human body.

3*dly*, He is made over again in the image of God, bearing his image as a child of the father, Col. iii. 10. And this comes to pass, in that the new creature being entirely sprung of Christ, being made by receiving from him grace for grace in him, must needs be his image, Gal. iv. 19. And he is the image of God; therefore it must be the image of God too. Thus Eve was made after God's image, but mediately, being made after Adam's image, who was made immediately after God's, Gen. ii. 18, margin, compared with 1 Cor. xi. 7, 8.

4thly, He becomes one spirit with Christ, which is the oneness with Christ that is the result of our uniting with him, 1 Cor. vi. 17, "He that is joined unto the Lord, is one spirit." The Spirit is the principal cause, faith the instrumental cause, joining or uniting us to Christ; but this is it whereby Christ and the believer formally coalesce or go together into one, viz. one spirit, *i. e.* one spiritual nature, Heb. ii. 11: even as Eve was one flesh with Adam, being made of him, of his flesh and bones; to which the Apostle alludes, Eph. v. 30. "For we are members of his body, of his flesh, and of his bones." Suppose a tree had a virtue of changing the graft into its own nature, as Christ has; the gardener ingrafts, the graff by his art unites close with the stock: then the stock conveys of its juice into the graff, whereby the nature of the graff is changed; here is the oneness arising from the uniting, they are one tree, of one nature. So the Spirit puts the soul to Christ, by faith it unites close with him: then Christ by his Spirit conveys of his graces to the soul, which change its nature into his own, and so they go into one, viz. one spiritual or divine nature, 2 Pet. i. 4, partaking of it with him, and that from him. So they are his seed, Is. liii. 10.

Lastly, He is put in a near capacity for all acts of holy obedience, whether in doing or suffering, Deut. xxx. 6; Heb. viii. 10; the seed of the several saving graces derived from Christ, and implanted in him, tending of their own nature to spring according to their several kinds. If the seed of any grace were wanting in him, then he would be in no near capacity for acting that grace wanting. Like as a dead man, who is not only quickened by a miracle, but is risen and come out of the grave, is in an immediate disposition for the common actions of life; so in this case of sanctification, the soul is not only quickened, as it is in effectual calling, but is in the nearest capacity to walk what way the Lord calls: Rom. vi. 4, "Therefore we are buried with him by baptism into death: that like as Christ was raised up from the dead by the glory of the Father, even so we also should walk in newness of life." In effectual calling, Christ says to the sinner, Arise; in sanctification he says, Loose him, and let him go.

2. But it is not a full measure of any grace that is then communicated from Christ by his Spirit to the believer: "For we know but in part," says the apostle Paul, 1 Cor. xiii. 9. And says the same apostle, Rom. vii. 23, "I see another law in my members, warring against the law of my mind, and bringing me into captivity to the

law of sin, which is in my members." The believer has derived to him from Christ, the graces of faith, love, &c. but none of them in perfection: even as when the child is perfectly formed in the womb, there is head, eyes, hands, feet, &c. but all of them very small, none of them come to perfection. Now, so far as they go, they do remove sin with its pollution off the soul: but they cannot fill up the room in any part; therefore there are remains of corruption in every part, mind, will, and affections, and the body in communion with the corrupt part, Rom. vii. 14.

Now, the consequent of this is an imperfection of sanctification: the believer is sanctified, but not perfectly sanctified. More particularly, hence,

1*st*, There two contrary principles in believers; the flesh and spirit, the new and old man, the new nature derived to them from the second Adam, the old unrenewed nature from the first Adam: the one the old inhabitant, the other the new incomer upon it; like the house of Saul, and the house of David, in Israel. Hence believers are a mystery to the world, yea to themselves: Can. vi. 13, "Return, return, O Shulamite, return, return, that we may look upon thee: what will ye see in the Shulamite? as it were the company of two armies." Rom. vii. 16, 17, "If then I do that which I would not, I consent unto the law, that it is good. Now then, it is no more I that do it, but sin that dwelleth in me.

2*dly*, There is a continual combat in them, between these two contrary principles, being together side for side, as it were, in every part: Gal. v. 17, "For the flesh lusteth against the Spirit, and the Spirit against the flesh: and these are contrary the one to the other; so that ye cannot do the things that ye would." Thus the believer is like Rebekah, Gen. xxv. 22, 23, who had the children struggling together within her; and who was told by the Lord, upon her inquiring into the affair, that two nations were in her womb, and two manner of people should be separated from her bowels. The two armies war in the Shulamite, Cant. vi. 13. So that the believer's heart by that means is often like a field of battle, where there is much confusion and struggle. There is something like this found sometimes in the unregenerate; but in them the struggle is between the flesh in one part lusting, and the flesh in another part fearing, 2 Pet. ii. 15, compared with Numb. xxii. 18. In the saints it is between the flesh and the spirit in one and the same part, receiving and refusing the same spiritual truth or falsehood, willing and nilling the same good or evil, of its own proper motion, Rom. vii. 15, 16, forecited.

3*dly*, Neither their good nor ill actions are carried to perfection,

Gal. v. 17, forecited. For the two contrary principles being thus yoked, neither of them gets its full swing. When grace prevails to carry the good point, yet corruption clogs it in some measure: and when corruption prevails, grace clogs it in some measure; Cant iv. 2, "Thy teeth are like a flock of sheep that are even shorn, which came up from the washing: whereof every one bear twins, and none is barren among them." Saints in heaven in good, and unregenerate men in evil, are like strong men travelling in a calm day; saints on earth, in good or ill, are like men travelling with a strong wind blowing in their face, that cannot make the way that otherwise they would.

3. Howbeit, it is a predominant measure of grace that is then conveyed by the Spirit from Christ to the soul: Rom. vi. 14, "For sin shall not have dominion over you: for ye are not under the law, but under grace." Grace is put in the heart to rule, though in midst of its enemies, which makes it difficult to maintain its superiority. Not that it is predominant in every particular event and encounter; experience testifies the contrary. Hence, says the apostle, Rom. vii. 23, "I see another law in my members, warring against the law of my mind, and bringing me into captivity to the law of sin, which is in my members." But it is fundamentally and habitually predominant; that is, it is more firmly rooted as an immortal seed against a mortal one, and generally speaking it prevails. Hence,

1*st*, The dominion and reigning power of sin is broken, Rom. vi. 14, forecited. It is turned off the throne it had before, and is put under the check of a superior principle. Hence the apostle saith, 1 John iii. 9, " Whosoever is born of God, doth not commit sin; for his seed remaineth in him: and he cannot sin, because he is born of God." Thus Christ delivers the soul from that enemy, to serve him. Hence is that of the prophet, Is. ix. 4, "Thou hast broken the yoke of his burden, and the staff of his shoulder, the rod of his oppressor, as in the day of Midian." Indwelling it may be for a time, and, as a troublesome guest, breed much disturbance in the house: but it is no more master of the house. This was typified by the remains of the Canaanites in the land, which Israel could not drive out, but yet brought them under tribute, Jud. i. 19, &c.

2*dly*, It shall be quite expelled at length: Rom. xvi. 20, "The God of peace shall bruise Satan under your feet shortly." Whatever particular battles it wons, the wars shall end in its ruin: 1 John v. 4, "Whatsoever is born of God, overcometh the world." When the true Israelite comes to the Red Sea of death, these

Egyptians shall be swallowed up there, and he shall see them all dead on the shore. Sin is crucified by the incoming of grace, and though the thief being on the cross may rage and blaspheme, yet shall he never come down till he breath out his last.

2*dly*, There is a continued application of the blood of Christ made to the believer by the Spirit, during his after continuing in the world. For the soul once united to Christ, his Spirit dwells in it ever after, never quits his dwelling. Hence Christ said to his disciples, John xiv. 16, 17, " I will pray the Father, and he shall give you another Comforter, that he may abide with you for ever; even the Spirit of truth, whom the world cannot receive, because it seeth him not, neither knoweth him : but ye know him, for he dwelleth with you, and shall be in you." And the Spirit continues that application to it from time to time till death, conveying fresh supplies of grace to it from Christ the head. Hence the grace of Christ conveyed to believers is held forth under the notion of a spring-well; John iv. 14, " But whosoever drinketh of the water that I shall give him, shall never thirst : but the water that I shall give him, shall be in him a well of water springing up into everlasting life ;" which is still affording new water. The fulness of grace in Christ is the spring-head, Col. ii. 19. The receivers into which it runs, are believers, his members, that receive supplies of grace from him, as the branches supplies of juice from the stock : John xv. 5, " I am the vine, ye are the branches : he that abideth in me, and I in him, the same bringeth forth much fruit." And the conveyer of these supplies from the head to the members, Philip i. 18, with ver. 11, is the Spirit. For clearing this purpose, consider,

1. Though one is renewed, and has the seed of all grace planted in him, in the begun application issuing in habitual sanctification ; yet he is not able of himself to exercise one grace, to wash off one remaining spot, or add to himself one stroke of purity : but thereto is necessary a new supply by the Spirit, 2 Cor. iii. 4, 5. Even of our gracious selves we can do nothing ; can bring forth no fruit of grace, John xv. 5, even when furnished with gracious qualities. This is not so very strange, if we consider, that though we have the power of natural motion, yet we cannot move a finger without a common providential influence of the Spirit, Acts xvii. 28, " For in him we live, and move, and have our being." Though fresh seed be cast into the earth, if the influence of the sun and rain is withheld, it springs not.

2. Hence every gracious act of ours is a fruit of the Spirit produced by him in us, through these supplies of grace ; as the springing of the seed is by the warmth and moisture it gets from the

heavens, Gal. v. 22, 23; Eph. v. 8. Hence the Spirit is said to lust against the flesh, Gal. v. 17, as producing these lustings in us; even as he is said to groan, Rom. viii. 26. So every act of mortification is by the Spirit, Rom. viii. 13, "If ye through the Spirit do mortify the deeds of the body, ye shall live." And so also is every act of obedience, Phil. ii. 13, "For it is God which worketh in you, both to will and to do of his good pleasure." So that take away the Spirit, and ye take away all true holiness.

3. These supplies of grace are given in such a measure only, in the continued application, as in the begun application. There is some measure of every grace supplied, Col. ii. 19. Hence, (Eph. v. 9.), "The fruit of the Spirit is in all goodness, and righteousness, and truth." But there is not a full measure of any grace: 1 Cor. xiii. 9, "For we know but in part." Yet there is a predominant measure, 2 Cor. xii. 9. Hence the imperfection of actual sanctification; there are still some spots to wash off while here. Washing of foul clothes will take time; there is much work for the hands there. But the washing of foul souls ordinarily takes more than the longest work of that kind. The Spirit could wash us perfectly clean in an instant, by a full application of the blood; but it is otherwise ordered. The thief on the cross was washed clean in a moment: but ordinarily the washing is gradual.

4. *Lastly*, These continued supplies of grace continue the washing of the soul; inasmuch as thereby,

1*st*, Inherent grace is preserved, that it die not out, amidst so many snares and temptations. It is but a created quality, and of itself would wither away and die out, and so leave the soul overwhelmed anew with the filth of sin, if it were not fed. Hence the Lord says, Is. xxvii. 3, "I the Lord do keep it, I will water it every moment; lest any hurt it, I will keep it night and day." John xv. 5, 6, "I am the vine, ye are the branches: He that abideth in me, and I in him, the same bringeth forth much fruit: for without me ye can do nothing. If a man abide not in me, he is cast forth as a branch, and is withered; and men gather them, and cast them into the fire, and they are burned." But the continued supplies from Christ by the Spirit, render it an abiding immortal seed, 1 Cor. i. 8, 9, compared with John xiv. 19; Jude ver. 1.

2*dly*, Inherent grace is excited, that it lie not idle, Cant. v. 4. Sometimes it lies like fire under the ashes; new supplies coming in by the Spirit, it is stirred up, and casts abroad its light in the soul. Hence the Spirit is compared to the wind, Cant. iv. 16. Being excited to action, it removes sin; as the stopt spring loosed, works out the mud. And,

3*dly*, It is increased and strengthened, that it may act more vigorously towards the expulsion of its enemy, Col. i. 10; Eph. iii. 16; Is. xl. 29. As an addition of soap makes the washing go on more thoroughly, so the fresh supplies of grace from Christ by the Spirit carry on the washing of the soul, causing the stream run higher to the carrying off more of the filth of sin, and beautifying the soul more.

3*dly*, There is a full application of the blood of Christ to the soul made by the Spirit at death. That moment the soul and body are separated, the Spirit brings in a full stream of grace from Christ into the soul, Eph. iii. 19. with 1 Cor. xiii. 8, 9, 10. The communication of grace which was before but in part, is then made perfect. For clearing of this purpose, note, that,

1. The perfection of grace taking place in the souls of believers at death, comes from the same spring as at conversion, and after, till death. It is all communicated to them from Christ their head, with this difference only, that the stream of it that ran small and scanty before, is then made to run full, as when a sluice is fully opened. As, out of his fulness, they got grace for grace in Christ, in some measure, before; so then, out of the same fulness, they get a fulness of grace for grace in him. For they grow to their perfection in him, as members of him, and therefore by communication from him, Eph. iv. 13. The new creature is both formed and perfected the same way.

2. It is the same Spirit who conveys the perfection of grace from Christ to believers at death, that conveyed the first grace, and the supplies thereof: the same Spirit who forms, and nourishes the new creature, in the time of this life, brings it to its perfection and full growth at death, Philip. i. 6; Psal. cxxxviii. 8. And as to the measure he then communicates.

1*st*, It is a full measure, such as wholly renews them in every part, perfecting the image of Christ, and so of God, on them, and utterly abolishes all remains of sin in them, 2 Cor. iv. 16, with Heb. xii. 23; Rev. vii. 14, 15. Thus they are washed perfectly clean, no spot is left in them, all being carried off by the full flood of grace conveyed then from Christ to them. And thus they are enabled to serve the Lord in perfection for ever, Rev. xxii. 3, with 1 Cor. xiii. 10.

2*dly*, Yet is it not such a measure, as that they never need more: no, but they will always be kept full, by the Spirit's communicating eternally to them full supplies of grace from Christ their head: Rev. vii. 17, "For the Lamb, which is in the midst of the throne, shall feed them, and shall lead them unto living fountains of waters: and God shall wipe away all tears from their eyes. Compared with John xvi. 14, "He shall glorify me: for he shall receive of mine, and shall shew it unto you." There will be nothing any more to stop or retard the flowing of grace from Christ into them; but the fountain will empty of its fulness into them without interruption. That there shall be such an eternal communication to them from Christ by the Spirit, is evident, in that they continue for ever members of Christ; and members cannot act but by continued communications of influences from their head: John xiv. 16, 17, "And I will pray the Father, and he shall give you another Comforter, that he may abide with you for ever; even the Spirit of truth, whom the world cannot receive, because it seeth him not, neither knoweth him: but ye know him, for he dwelleth with you, and shall be in you." John xv. 4, 5, "Abide in me, and I in you. As the branch cannot bear fruit of itself, except it abide in the vine; no more can ye, except ye abide in me. I am the vine, ye are the branches: He that abideth in me, and I in him, the same bringeth forth much fruit: for without me ye can do nothing."

From what is said on this head, we draw these inferences.

1. They are not washed from their filthiness, that have never had a discovery of the filth of sin made to them by the Spirit. Men may get a sight of the guilt of sin, that will fill them with fear and terror; that yet get no kindly sight of the filth of sin, filling them with shame and self-loathing before the Lord. But without this last, there is no sanctification: Ezek. xxxvi. 31, "Then shall ye remember your own evil ways, and your doings that were not good, and shall loathe yourselves in your own sight, for your iniquities, and for your abominations." Therefore never think ye have seen sin aright, till ye see it in the monstrous filthiness of it, as opposite to the holiness of God: it is that only will turn one's stomach on it, and cause them to vomit it up by true repentance.

2. The filthiness of the soul by sin, is never duly seen, till it appear so ingrained as nothing but the blood of Christ can wash it off. They evidence but slight thoughts of the filth of sin, that think it can be carried off by prayers, confessions, tears, and outward reformation: therefore the Spirit carries the elect beyond all these to the laver of Christ's blood. Hence David prayed, Psal. li. 2, "Wash me throughly from mine iniquity, and cleanse me from my sin." There only is there merit and efficacy sufficient to wash out the pollution.

3. Whosoever truly come to Christ by faith, they come to him for sanctification, as well as justification; that they may be washed from the filth of sin by him, as well as freed from the guilt of sin

through him. Hence faith is a coming to the waters, Is. lv. 1, and that to be washed in them, Zech. xiii. 1. It is but false faith that looks to Christ for freedom from guilt and the wrath of God, and not for conformity to God in holiness.

4. For to stand off from Christ, and uniting with him by believing on him, till one has made himself clean and fit for Christ, is the work of a false heart, marring the soul's washing; not the work of the Spirit, carrying on the washing of the soul. For it is the work of the Spirit to put the unclean soul in the laver, uniting it to Christ, that it may be made clean. Therefore let no pollution of sin whatsoever keep you back from Christ; but let the consideration of your pollution drive you forward to him; and the greater it is, ye have the more need to make speed, and unite the more closely with Christ.

5. Whosoever are united to Christ by the Spirit, are sanctified persons, truly regenerate, new creatures: 2 Cor. v. 17, " If any man be in Christ, he is a new creature : old things are passed away, behold, all things are become new." In vain do men pretend to be members of Christ, while they remain unsanctified in their nature and life. Can one be united to Christ in whom the fulness of grace is lodged, and yet there be no communication of grace from him to them? or can there be such a communication, and yet they not be renewed after his image? and if a new nature, must there not be a new life?

6. *Lastly*, True Christianity is in its own nature a progressive thing, going towards perfection. Hence says the apostle, Philip iii. 12, " Not as though I had already attained, either were already perfect: but I follow after, if that I may apprehend that for which also I am apprehended of Christ Jesus." It is a most dismal sign, where a person having, as he thinks, embraced Christ for salvation, and so secured himself for eternity, is no further careful to advance in practical religion, but continues easy, being at a stand; seeing " the path of the just is as the shining light, that shineth more and more unto the perfect day," Prov. iv. 18. It is true, a real believer may not only be at a stand for a while, but may be going back : but it is of the nature of grace, as of a seed, or the morning light, to go forward and increase till it come to perfection, John iv. 14; Eph. iv. 13. This is the result of the continued application of the blood of Christ to the believer by the Spirit. Therefore observe whether ye grow or not.

Thirdly, Christ washeth sinners through faith. Hence the apostle, Acts xv. 9, speaks of " purifying the heart by faith;" and xxvi. 18, of being sent to open men's eyes, " and to turn them from darkness to light, and from the power of Satan unto God, that they may receive forgiveness of sins, and inheritance among them which are sanctified by faith that is in Christ." And faith has that place in the washing of defiled souls, that the hand of the party washed hath in the washing of himself, under the management of the principal washer. For faith is the hand of the soul, John i. 12. And in the spiritual washing it is active. The soul being first passively washed by the Spirit, washeth itself by faith; being put into the laver by the Spirit, it applies the water by faith, 2 Cor. vii. 1. Yet Christ by his Spirit is still the principal cause of the washing; forasmuch as he both works faith in the soul, and then by new influences puts it in exercise: Philip. ii. 13, "For it is God which worketh in us, both to will and to do of his good pleasure." And so faith is the instrumental cause of our washing from sin, Acts xv. 9, forecited.

Now, the efficacy of faith in the washing of the soul lies in these following things, under these two heads.

1. It is the eye of the soul in that matter, and so it is an impulsive cause moving the sinner to wash away his sin, Gal. ii. 16; and is supposed in such calls, as that Is. i. 16, "Wash ye, make you clean, put away the evil of your doings from before mine eyes, cease to do evil, learn to do well." Now, by the eye of faith,

1*st*, The man discerns his pollution, that he is all over defiled, and unlike God: Is. lxiv. 6, "We are all as an unclean thing, and all our righteousnesses are as filthy rags, and we all do fade as a leaf, and our iniquities, like the wind, have taken us away." He looks into the glass of the word, which is a representation of God's holiness, and so represents the sinner as vile and loathsome. The man believes the representation to be true, and so cries out, as Job xl. 4, "Behold, I am vile, what shall I answer thee? I will lay mine hand upon my mouth." This glass is held to the eyes of others; but, notwithstanding being unbelievers, they see not their universal pollution. But thus the believer sees the need of washing.

2*dly*, He discerns the depth of the stain, that it can be washed out by no human art. Faith brings, from the testimony of the word, that report into the soul, Jer. ii. 22, "For though thou wash thee with nitre, and take thee much soap, yet thine iniquity is marked before me, saith the Lord God." Unbelievers are ruined in their pollution for want of this; they see not how deep their defilement lies; so they think their own nitre and soap will do their business, that Abana and Pharpar may cleanse the leper, as well as any other water, Hos. v. 13. But faith sees them all physicians of no value: and so the believer sees the need of another laver even the blood of Christ.

3*dly*, He discerns the ill of his pollution on the one hand, and the good of the washing on the other. By faith the man is persuaded of the destructive nature of sin, and its contrariety to God's nature and will: and he is persuaded too of the beauty and excellency of holiness, or purification from sin. The one he sees in the glass of the law, its threatenings and commands; the other in the glass of the gospel, in the face of Jesus. And these are a spur to incite him to seek to be washed, Luke xv. 17, 18.

4*thly*, He discerns the laver, Christ crucified, Is. xlv. 22. By the help of the glass of the gospel, he takes up the sea of Christ's blood, as the only laver for unclean souls, Matth. ix. 20, 21. And by faith the unclean soul discerns Christ the laver,

(1.) As an efficacious laver in all cases, 1 John i. 7, "The blood of Jesus Christ cleanseth us from all sin." The man believes that Christ is able to wash out the deepest stain, to make the filthiest soul clean, according to the word, Is. i. 18, "Come now, and let us reason together, saith the Lord: though your sins be as scarlet, they shall be as white as snow; though they be red like crimson, they shall be as wool." This is necessary, as appears in the case of the blind men, Matth. ix. 28, 29, "Jesus saith unto them, Believe ye that I am able to do this? they said unto him, Yea, Lord. Then touched he their eyes, saying, According to your faith, be it unto you."

(2.) As an open laver in its own case, Zech. xiii. 1, "In that day there shall be a fountain opened to the house of David, and to the inhabitants of Jerusalem, for sin, and for uncleanness." Compared with Heb. xi. 6, "But without faith it is impossible to please him: for he that cometh to God, must believe that he is, and that he is a rewarder of them that diligently seek him." This is believing the gospel, one's warrant to come to Christ, without which none can come. For if one should look on the fountain as open to all the world, but only sealed to him, this will effectually mar his access to it, Jer. ii. 25, "Thou saidst, There is no hope. No, for I have loved strangers, and after them will I go." But faith says, Psal. lxv. 3, "Iniquities prevail against me: as for our transgressions, thou shalt purge them away."

2. Faith is the hand of the soul in that matter, and so it is an instrumental cause of washing away sin. And by the hand of faith,

1*st*, The soul embraceth Christ, and unites with him: John i. 12, "But as many as received him, to them gave he power to become the sons of God, even to them that believe on his name." Compared with Eph. iii. 17, "That Christ may dwell in your hearts by faith." The soul, at its first union with Christ, being plunged into the laver by the Spirit, doth by faith spread out itself therein; as one who having jumped into the water to swim, doth immediately spread out his body in it, and embrace the water as it were. Christ having apprehended the unclean soul by his Spirit, and united it passively to himself; the soul again apprehends him by faith, and actively unites with him. And hereby faith brings in the first application of his blood, the effect of which is habitual sanctification.

2*dly*, The soul cleaveth to Christ, and abideth in him, all along till death: Heb. x. 39, "But we are not of them who draw back unto perdition; but of them that believe, to the saving of the soul." It is never extinguished again in the soul; though its gripe may be sometime slacked, yet it never lets it quite go: Luke xxii. 32, "But I have prayed for thee, that thy faith fail not." Hereby it brings in the continued application, for progressive sanctification, John xv. 5. And the stronger its gripes are at any time, the more plentiful application is there of the blood of Christ to the soul; as the stronger the child sucks, he draws out the more milk, Is. lxvi. 11. Hence he that has the strongest faith, hath the holiest heart and life.

3*dly*, The soul cleaveth to Christ in death. When the body is falling down, the man still cleaves to and abides in Christ, and so dying in faith, dies in the Lord, Heb. xi. 13; Rev. xiv. 13. Faith keeps the gripe of Christ, while the soul is losing gripe of the body; and as the body drops off, it brings in a full application of Christ's blood, which perfects sanctification. So the soul drops the remains of sin together with the body.

Now, the instrumental efficacy of faith for the washing of the soul, lies in trust: and as it trusts, it purifies; for therein lies its nature, and therefore its efficacy comes that way, Psal. xxxi. 19; Psal. xxxvii. 40. And the object of that trust is twofold.

(1.) The object of this trust is real, viz. the word. Faith trusts or believes the word as firm and infallible truth. Hence the apostle, 2 Thess. ii. 13, speaks of the belief of the truth. Faith trusts or believes particularly the word of the promise of the gospel, holding out to sinners the benefit of sanctification as well as other benefits, 2 Cor. vii. 1; such as that promise, Ezek. xxxvi. 25, "I will sprinkle clean water upon you, and ye shall be clean: from all your filthiness, and from all your idols will I cleanse you." This trust of the word of the gospel is our original obedience to the truth, 1 Pet. i. 22, wherein the soul subjects itself wholly to the truth of God in his word, believing it over the belly of all objections in this point, saying, as Mic. vii. 19, "He will turn again, he will have compassion upon us: he will subdue our iniquities: and thou wilt cast all their sins into the depths of the sea."

(2.) The object of this trust is personal, viz. Christ himself. The soul trusts on Christ for the washing of it. Hence is that invitation, Is. xlv. 22, "Look unto me, and be ye saved, all the ends of the earth: for I am God, and there is none else." And hence is the language of faith, Psal. lxv. 3, "Iniquities prevail against me: as for our transgressions, thou shalt purge them away." It is the very nature of faith to renounce all confidence in other things, and to trust in him alone for the washing of the soul. Hence Paul saith, Philip iii. 3, "We are the circumcision, which worship God in the spirit, and rejoice in Christ Jesus, and have no confidence in the flesh." In the word of promise he is held forth as "the Lamb of God taking away the sin of the world," as made sanctification to us: and faith is a trust or reliance on him as such to us, John i. 12. But more particularly,

Faith's trust on Christ is on him as crucified. Hence the apostle saith, 1 Cor. ii. 2, "I determined not to know any thing, save Jesus Christ, and him crucified." While we look on him simply as God, we see his justice flaming against sin, and barring all sanctifying influences: Heb. xii. 29, "For our God is a consuming fire." But looking on him as God-man, by his obedience and death making satisfaction for sin, we have a fit object of trust for our sanctification; for there we see a fulness of merit for purging away sin, Rom. vi. 6, "Knowing this, that our old man is crucified with him, that the body of sin might be destroyed, that henceforth we should not serve sin."

Hence faith has a particular eye to the blood of Christ, in the point of sanctification, as well as justification. Hence the apostle saith, Rom. iii. 25, "God hath set him forth to be a propitiation, through faith in his blood, to declare his righteousness for the remission of sins." And again, Heb. ix. 14, "The blood of Christ, who, through the eternal Spirit, offered himself without spot to God, shall purge your conscience from dead works to serve the living God: that being the immediate cause of our washing, as the blood of his sacrifice offered to God for atonement, and sprinkled on us for our purification, Heb. xii. 24.

Now, this trust for washing, placed on Christ crucified held forth to us in the word of promise, which is that wherein the efficacy of faith for sanctifying us instrumentally lies, may be taken up in these four things.

[1.] The soul's turning its eye of expectation of purification, from off all things else, and fixing it on Christ crucified. Hence is the gospel invitation, Is. xlv. 22, "Look unto me, and be ye saved, all the ends of the earth: for I am God, and there is none else." (Heb.) Face unto me. Secure sinners, being indifferent about holiness, look no where for it; they desire it not. Awakened sinners look for it to physicians of no value, such as their own endeavours, resolutions, &c. But faith looks off from all creatures, means, &c., unto Christ alone, for it, as the woman with the bloody issue did, Mark v. 25—28, that virtue may come from him for purifying.

[2.] Applying the promise of spiritual washing to itself: 2 Cor. vii. 1, "Having these promises, let us cleanse ourselves from all filthiness of the flesh and spirit, perfecting holiness in the fear of God." The word holds forth the promise of cleansing from sin, to sinners indefinitely, saying, as Ezek. xxxvi. 25, "I will sprinkle clean water upon you, and ye shall be clean: from all your filthiness, and from all your idols will I cleanse you." Faith catches hold of it, and brings it home, saying, as Psal. lxv. 3, "Iniquities prevail against me: as for our transgressions, thou shalt purge them away." Mic. vii. 19, "He will turn again, he will have compassion upon us: he will subdue our iniquities: and thou wilt cast all their sins into the depths of the sea." It pleads the promise, and hangs by it. Particularly, it appropriates the privilege of legal freedom, Rom. vi. 10, 11, "For in that he died, he died unto sin once: but in that he liveth, he liveth unto God. Likewise reckon ye also yourselves to be dead indeed unto sin; but alive unto God through Jesus Christ our Lord:" so that thereby the soul looks on itself as dead in point of right and privilege to sin, Rom. vi. 2, "How shall we that are dead to sin, live any longer therein?"

[3.] Relying on the merit of Christ for the out-making of the promise of sanctification, saying, as Psal. li. 7, "Purge me with hyssop, and I shall be clean: wash me, and I shall be whiter than snow." Compared with 1 John i. 7, "The blood of Jesus Christ cleanseth us from all sin." The soul sees it is a great privilege as well as a duty, and believes that God will make it holy, for Christ's sake, forasmuch as he died for that very end, Tit. ii. 14. For true faith has the same reliance on Christ for sanctification as for justification, knowing that the one is the purchase of the Redeemer's blood, even as the other.

[4.] *Lastly*, Acquiescing in the faithfulness of God in his word, for that effect. Faith receives the word of promise for sanctification; and says, with Mary, Luke i. 38, "Be it unto me according to thy word." The purification of the soul from sin has so many difficulties about it, that the sinner truly sensible accounts it impossible in respect of all created power: but since God has said, that he will do it, the soul acquiesces in his word, judging him faithful who hath promised, Rom. iv. 24; Heb. xi. 11.

This faith or trust purifies from sin, according to the scripture, and the experience of the saints: Acts xv. 9, "Purifying their hearts by faith." Hereto agrees the Psalmist's experience, Psal.

xxviii. 7, "The Lord is my strength and my shield, my heart trusted in him, and I am helped: therefore my heart greatly rejoiceth, and with my song will I praise him." And so does that of those to whom Peter wrote, and of whom he says, 1 Pet. i. 22, "Ye have purified your souls in obeying the truth through the Spirit." Yea, by this trust, joy is brought into the soul, as vers. 8, 9, "Whom having not seen, ye love; in whom though now ye see him not, yet believing, ye rejoice with joy unspeakable, and full of glory; receiving the end of your faith, even the salvation of your souls." Rom. xv. 13, "Now the God of hope fill you with all joy and peace in believing, that ye may abound in hope through the power of the Holy Ghost." And that pre-supposeth the purging of the soul from sin, Is. xxxiii. 24, "The inhabitant shall not say, I am sick: the people that dwell therein shall be forgiven their iniquity."

QUESTION. How has that trust that efficacy? ANSWER. By the appointment of God. How had the looking to the brazen serpent such efficacy as to cure the stung Israelites, but by God's appointment? So is the case here: John iii. 14, 15, 16, "As Moses lifted up the serpent in the wilderness, even so must the Son of man be lifted up: that whosoever believeth in him, should not perish, but have eternal life. For God so loved the world, that he gave his only begotten Son, that whosoever believeth in him, should not perish, but have everlasting life." The nature and efficacy of saving faith may be learned in part from that of the faith of miracles, they agreeing in one general kind. Matth. ix. 28, 29, 30, "Jesus saith unto the blind men, Believe ye that I am able to do this? they said unto him, Yea, Lord. Then touched he their eyes, saying, According to your faith, be it unto you. And their eyes were opened." God has made choice of faith or trust for that end, and given it a word of appointment, Mark xvi. 16, "He that believeth shall be saved." And the appointment is, that on the soul's so trusting in Christ, the soul shall be sanctified by the Spirit with the blood, Gal. iii. 2. And there is a fitness in the appointment of this as a mean for,

(1.) Faith trusts the word of God, and the faithfulness of God requires that it be accomplished to them that trust it. So it is secured, Rom. ix. 33, "Whosoever believeth on him, shall not be ashamed." If you would have a benefit from an honest man, you cannot take a more effectual way to obtain it, than, having got his word for it, to trust it, plead it, and hold him to it.

(2.) Christ himself with all his benefits, comes to us in the word. Hence the apostle saith, Rom. x. 6, 7, 8, "The righteousness which is of faith, speaketh on this wise, Say not in thine heart, Who shall ascend into heaven? (that is, to bring Christ down from above); or, Who shall descend into the deep? (that is, to bring up Christ again from the dead): but what saith it? The word is nigh thee, even in thy mouth, and in thy heart: that is the word of faith which we preach." Trusting the word is the only effectual way of receiving it farther than into the ears, at least as it is a promise. So receiving the word by faith, we receive Christ, and consequently the purifying virtue of his blood that is in it, with himself. Hence the apostle saith of the Thessalonians, 1 Thess. ii. 13, "For this cause also thank we God without ceasing, because when ye received the word of God which ye heard of us, ye received it not as the word of men, but (as it is in truth) the word of God, which effectually worketh also in you that believe." And then,

(3.) There is nothing so adapted to the end of glorifying free grace, as this trust of faith is; and that is the great end of the gospel: Rom. iv. 16, "Therefore it is of faith, that it might be by grace; to the end the promise might be sure to all the seed."

I shall shut up this branch with a few inferences.

INFERENCE 1. That is not true faith that leaves the soul still unholy, lying in the filth of sin. Unwashed sinners are unbelievers certainly: Tit. i. 15, "Unto the pure all things are pure: but unto them that are defiled, and unbelieving, is nothing pure; but even their mind and conscience is defiled." In vain will ye please yourselves with a conceit of your believing in Christ, while your pretended faith brings in no sanctifying influences into your souls: James ii. 14, "What doth it profit, though a man say he hath faith, and have not works? can faith save him?" True faith, according to the scripture, hath a double effect.

1*st*, Within, faith purifies the heart, Acts xv. 9, and makes it evangelically clean, Psal. xxiv. 3, 4. It breaks the reigning power of lusts within, maintains a combat against their broken forces, sets the soul to approve itself to God in the inner man, where no eye sees, and longs for and presseth toward perfection.

2*dly*, Without, faith works by love, in all duties of piety towards God, and justice and mercy towards our neighbour: Gal. v. 6, "For in Jesus Christ, neither circumcision availeth any thing, nor uncircumcision, but faith which worketh by love." It is a principle within, that casts abroad its cleansing efficacy into the life, purifying men's words and actions.

INFERENCE 2. Then whosoever are really washed from their sins, as they will be sure to use all means of holiness, yet they will be carried beyond them all to Christ for it. They will be conscientious in the practice of holy duties, and so go beyond the profane and careless; and yet they will not rest in them, but quit them all in point of confidence when they have done, and so go beyond hypocrites: "For," saith the apostle, Phil. iii. 3, "we are the circumcision, which worship God in the spirit, and rejoice in Christ Jesus, and have no confidence in the flesh." This is the little further that the spouse went, Cant. iii. 4. and so found her beloved.

INFERENCE 3. *Lastly*, The only true way to be holy, is to believe in Christ. This is the way that all the members of Christ are sanctified; they are sanctified in him, 1 Cor. i. 2, through faith, Acts xxvi. 18. And there is no true holiness in subjects capable of faith, without it: for saith Christ, John xv. 5, "Without me ye can do nothing." So if the soul be brought to faith in Christ, it will undoubtedly be made holy: if it be not, all other means of washing of a person will be but washing a blackmoor, that will never become white for them all.

Thus far of those things which Christ useth more immediately for washing sinners.

Secondly, There are other means which Christ useth for that purpose, more mediately: of which briefly.

First, Christ washeth sinners by the word, Eph. v. 26. Hence Christ saith of his disciples, John xv. 3, "Now ye are clean through the word which I have spoken unto you." And hence he prays to his Father, John xvii. 17, "Sanctify them through thy truth: thy word is truth." The word written, read, and preached, is the great external mean of washing sinners; and is effectual for that end by the energy of the Spirit, being received by faith. The use of the word to the washing of the sinner lies in these things following.

1. It is the glass wherein the filthy sinner discerns his spots and filthiness. The word of the law particularly is that glass: Rom. iii. 20, "For by the law is the knowledge of sin." It represents to men the sinfulness of their nature, hearts, and lives: and when Christ comes to wash a sinner, he holds that glass to his eyes to convince him of sin, by the Spirit. Therefore the Psalmist recommends it to young men, Psal. cxix. 9, "Wherewith shall a young man cleanse his way? by taking heed thereto according to thy word." And they that look not into the word for this end, care not for washing.

2. It is a spur to washing, an external impulsive cause, by the strong motives whereby it presseth the sinner to wash. Here the law presseth him by its threatenings and curses against the un-

clean; the gospel presseth with the possibility, excellency, and unspeakable advantage of washing.

3. It is the key that sets open the fountain for washing in, Zech. xiii. 1, "In that day there shall be a fountain opened to the house of David, and to the inhabitants of Jerusalem, for sin, and for uncleanness." It is opened by the preaching of the gospel; which shews sinners, that whatever be their pollution, they are welcome to it. The voice of Christ in the gospel is, "Behold me," Is. lxv. 1, *i. e.* "Here I am." Thereby our Lord unlocks his treasures, laying them open to the view of sinners.

4. It is the vehicle of the blood and Spirit of Christ, whereby sinners may be washed, receiving the word by faith, Rom. x. 6, 7, 8, forecited. John vi. 63, "It is the spirit that quickeneth, the flesh profiteth nothing: the words that I speak unto you, they are spirit, and they are life." The gospel is therefore called "the ministration of the Spirit, and righteousness," 2 Cor. iii. inasmuch as thereby Christ communicates his Spirit to sinners, and brings righteousness to them. Hence receiving the word by faith, the soul is cast into the mould of it, Rom. vi. 17: for it is able to save the soul, Jam. i. 21, and works effectually in it, 1 Thess. ii. 13. to the cleansing of the soul, John xv. 3, "Now ye are clean through the word which I have spoken unto you."

I shall shut up this branch also with a few inferences.

INFERENCE 1. Saints and sinners need the word; forasmuch as they are both defiled, and need washing; the one washing to be begun on them, and the other to be carried on. And they that can live contented without it, are content to lie still in their filthiness; and will need no more to ruin them, but to get their will.

INFERENCE 2. They have an enmity at the word, appearing in their aversion to dip into it, and neglect of it, are neither washed, nor desire to be washed: Job xxi. 14, "Therefore they say unto God, Depart from us; for we desire not the knowledge of thy ways." The reason of their enmity against it is, their love to their lusts, to which it is an enemy: as, on the contrary, they whose hearts are turned against sin, are turned towards the word, as a mean for purging it away: John iii. 20, 21, "For every one that doth evil, hateth the light, neither cometh to the light, lest his deeds should be reproved. But he that doth truth, cometh to the light, that his deeds may be made manifest, that they are wrought in God."

INFERENCE 3. Their soul's case is very hopeless, who get no good of the word: and these are all such who get no conviction by it, or are not stirred up by it to seek to be purged from their filthiness, who are not pointed to Christ as the only laver, and never partake of his blood and Spirit, by it. These are they on whom the great mean of washing from sin is ineffectual; of whom the Lord may justly say, as Ezek. xxiv. 13, "In thy filthiness is lewdness: because I have purged thee, and thou wast not purged, thou shalt not be purged from thy filthiness any more, till I have caused my fury to rest upon thee."

INFERENCE 4. *Lastly,* They do not believe the word, who are not cleansed in heart and life thereby; for (as the apostle saith of the Thessalonians, 1 Thess. ii. 13,) "When ye received the word of God which ye heard of us, ye received it not as the word of men, but (as it is in truth) the word of God, which effectually worketh also in you that believe." If the word were received by faith, it could not miss to be sanctifying: but beholding the unholiness of men, we may cry out, as Is. liii. 1, "Who hath believed our report? and to whom is the arm of the Lord revealed?" The word preached is not truly believed, therefore it brings not forth fruit.

Secondly, Christ washeth sinners by the sacraments, Eph. v. 26. Hence baptism is said to save us, 1 Pet. iii. 21. The sacraments are external means of spiritual washing, and are made effectual by the Spirit, being received by faith; but no otherwise in subjects capable of believing; for God hath not communicated the virtue of sanctifying to the elements as to natural causes which work necessarily, 1 Pet. iii. 21.

The use of the sacraments to the washing of sinners lies here.

1. The sacraments point out to us the laver wherein we may be washed, as being representing signs of Christ with his sanctifying blood. Hence the apostle saith, 1 Cor. x. 16, "The cup of blessing which we bless, is it not the communion of the blood of Christ? The bread which we break, is it not the communion of the body of Christ?" They set the laver as it were before our eyes, and call us to think of it, and our need thereof. Therein Christ is as it were crucified before our eye, his blood springing forth for our washing.

2. The sacraments confirm our right in it, and our welcome to it, as seals. Hence the apostle saith concerning Abraham, Rom. iv. 11, "He received the sign of circumcision, a seal of the righteousness of faith which he had yet being uncircumcised: that he might be the father of all them that believe, though they be not circumcised; that righteousness might be imputed unto them also." The blood of Christ is most precious; but there is a grant of it made to us in the word, which is our charter, and the sacraments seal it. The word says, John iii. 16, "God so loved the world, that he gave his only begotten Son, that whosoever believeth in him, should not perish, but have everlasting life:" the sacraments seal it, that so we

may be excited and encouraged to come boldly, and make use of it for our sanctification.

3. The sacraments present, exhibit, and apply it to us who believe, 1 Cor. xi. 24. As by earth and stone delivered to a man upon a legal right, he is infefted and possessed of the house or land: so, by the sacraments received by faith, Christ and all his benefits are applied to us, for our cleansing.

An inference shall shut up this branch.

INFERENCE. Hence we may try, whether the sacraments be effectual to us, or not; whether we have believingly received them or not. While people are never the more holy, for all the sacraments they receive, the more the worse, their disease is the more confirmed their filthiness is the more fixed on them. But when they stir up the soul to an usemaking of Christ for sanctification, and men get a cubit added to their spiritual stature, it is a good sign.

Thirdly, and *Lastly*, Christ washeth sinners by afflictions. Hence the prophet saith, Is. xxvii. 9, "By this therefore shall the iniquity of Jacob be purged, and this is all the fruit to take away his sin." They also are but external means, in the hand of the Spirit, and cannot of themselves purify. But the Spirit makes use of them for cleansing sinners. There are two ways of purging filthiness, by water, and by fire; as we learn from Is. iv. 4, "When the Lord shall have washed away the filth of the daughters of Zion, and shall have purged the blood of Jerusalem from the midst thereof, by the spirit of judgment, and by the spirit of burning." Afflictions are God's fire for that end. Their use in the washing is sixfold.

1. Afflictions are memorials of ours in, and so puts us in mind to look back on our defilements; as they were to Joseph's brethren, when they said, as Gen. xlii. 21, "We are verily guilty concerning our brother, in that we saw the anguish of his soul, when he besought us; and we would not hear: therefore is this distress come upon us." The prosperous sinner wallows at ease in his filthiness; but when God lays his afflicting hand on him, the sharper it is, conscience is readily the more awakened out of its sleep. And it will readily read the sin, out of the punishment.

2. Afflictions are a glass, wherein one sees the loathsomeness of sin in the sight of God. While the sinner prospers in his course, he cannot think that God is sore displeased at it; as the Lord himself saith unto the sinner, Psal. l. 21, "These things hast thou done, and I kept silence: thou thoughtest that I was altogether such a one as thyself." But affliction is such a token of God's displeasure against sin, that when it comes, the sinner alters his thoughts; sees its loathsomeness before God, and therefore loathsome in itself; which makes him anxious to be washed.

3. Afflictions are a fire that melt off the paint, and deface the beauty of the defiling objects in the world. Hence saith the Lord unto Israel, Jer. ii. 36, 37, "Why gaddest thou about so much to change thy way? thou also shalt be ashamed of Egypt, as thou wast ashamed of Assyria. Yea, thou shalt go forth from him, and thine hands upon thine head: for the Lord hath rejected thy confidences, and thou shalt not prosper in them." Where was the excellency of the thirty pieces when God's hand was lifted up against Judas for them? The beauty of former lusts melts away, when a man is laid on a sick-bed: and the bewitching creature then loses all its charms.

4. Afflictions are a bridle whereby men are restrained from defiling themselves more, and are brought to a stand in a defiling course. Hence the Lord saith unto Israel, Hos. ii. 6, "Behold, I will hedge up thy way with thorns, and make a wall, that she shall not find her paths." They serve to take off the edge of corrupt affections, and make them to languish; whereby the sinner becomes more considerate, and pliable to counsel from the word.

5. Afflictions are occasional causes of sinners thinking of and going to the fountain to wash. Hence the Lord saith of Israel, Hos. v. 15, "I will go and return to my place, till they acknowledge their offence, and seek my face: in their afflictions they will seek me early." How many are there to whom afflictions have been the blessed means and occasions of their turning serious? Such a rod they met with, or they had gone on like the wild ass upon the mountains, snuffing up the wind.

6. *Lastly*, Afflictions are a sharp wind to blow up the fire of grace where it is, and particularly to excite faith, whereby the soul is washed. Hence the spouse prayeth, Cant. iv. 16, "Awake, O north-wind, and come, thou south, blow upon my garden, that the spices thereof may flow out." In prosperity people can fetch in their comfort by sense; but in afflictions, when created streams are dried up, they must fetch it in by faith, or else want it.

Two inferences shall conclude this branch.

INFERENCE 1. Let this cause us to take afflictions kindly; since they are means by which Christ washeth us. Though the water be cold and piercing, yet we endure it, that we may get our hands made clean. Though medicines sicken us, we blame not the physician, because they are for our health. Why should we be angry at our God afflicting us, since the fruit designed is to purge away sin?

INFERENCE 2. Let us, in all our afflictions, seek purification from our sin, and know they are not effectual unless they have a sanctifying efficacy on us. They are indeed of the nature of fire, first causing the scum to come above, but next throwing it off. They do discover much of the corruption of the heart, that otherwise would be latent: but then if they humble the soul under a sense of sinfulness, and send it anew to Christ for purging of the nature, they are not in vain.

I shall now proceed to the second general head proposed, namely,

II. To consider the unwashed or unsanctified sinner's having no part with Christ.

In discussing this head, I shall shew,

1. What the unwashed sinner's having no part with Christ supposeth; and,

2. Wherein it lies.

First, We shall shew what the unwashed sinner's having no part with Christ supposeth. It supposeth,

1. That Christ himself is happy. He is not only happy as he is God, Rom. ix. 5, who is therefore styled "God blessed for ever;" but as he is Mediator, the head of the body, the church. Hence it is said of him, Psal. lxxii. 17, "Men shall be blessed in him, all nations shall call him blessed." All mankind were brought to misery and ruin by Adam's fall: but the man Christ was an exception from that rule. He was happy from the moment of the incarnation, all along, notwithstanding what he suffered: and from his resurrection and ascension his happiness was completed: Phil. ii. 9, "Wherefore God also hath highly exalted him, and given him a name which is above every name." Heb. x. 13, "From henceforth expecting till his enemies be made his footstool." There are two things wherein Christ is completely happy.

1*st*, In having fully done the work he undertook to do. Hence he says to his Father, John xvii. 4, "I have glorified thee on the earth: I have finished the work which thou gavest me to do." He had a great work to do, for the glory of his Father, and the salvation of sinners. It was the hardest work that ever was taken in hand. All hardships from heaven, earth, and hell, met together upon him; and his work was to go through them all in a course of perfect obedience. And now it is done; he was born holy, lived righteous, satisfied completely by his death: now he is got to the joy set before him: Rom. vi. 9, "Christ being raised from the dead, dieth no more; death hath no more dominion over him." Rev. iii. 21, "To him that overcometh will I grant to sit with me in my throne, even as I also overcame, and am set down with my Father in his throne."

2*dly*, In having received the reward of his work. Our Lord, "for the joy that was set before him, endured the cross, despising the shame, and is set down at the right hand of the throne of God," Heb. xii. 2. Never was there such a reward of work, as Christ has received; it bears proportion to the work, which was of infinite value. All the promises of the covenant, whether respecting himself, or his people, are now in his hand. They are won by him, and he is put in possession of the things promised, which make an inexhaustible treasure. Hence the apostle, (Eph. iii. 8.) speaks of "the unsearchable riches of Christ."

2. There is enough in him to make others happy too: Col. i. 19, "For it pleased the Father, that in him should all fulness dwell." There is a fulness of a fountain in him, whereby others may be supplied from him, may have part with him, and yet he have no lack. The first Adam was a spring of ruin to all his posterity: but the gospel points out Christ the second Adam as a spring of happiness for wretched sinners.

3. Sinners may have part with Christ in his fulness; it is lodged in him to be communicated. Hence our Lord himself says, Matth. xi. 27, 28, "All things are delivered unto me of my Father: and no man knoweth the Son but the Father: neither knoweth any man the Father, save the Son, and he to whomsoever the Son will reveal him. Come unto me, all ye that labour, and are heavy laden, and I will give you rest." He is the bowl on the top of the candlestick, (Zech. iv. 2.) the immediate receptacle of the oil, from whence it is conveyed to the seven lamps. Joseph was sent to Egypt, and exalted there, to provide for Jacob's family in the dearth: so Christ is great Steward of heaven, for the behoof of poor sinners; that he having all in his hand, they may be happy in having part with him.

4. All that are sanctified are happy in having part with Christ: Col. ii. 9, 10, "For in him dwelleth all the fulness of the Godhead bodily. And ye are complete in him." They have part in his work, by imputation; even as they had part with Adam in his sin: Rom. v. 19, "For as by one man's disobedience many were made sinners: so by the obedience of one, shall many be made righteous." They have part in his reward, by a real communication thereof to them; even as they had part with Adam in the corruption of his nature: John i. 16, "And of his fulness have all we received, and grace for grace." 1 Cor. xv. 22, "For as in Adam all die, even so in Christ shall all be made alive." This, it is true, is but imperfect as yet; but it is so begun that it will undoubtedly be perfected. But such as it is, their sanctification is not the cause of it, but it is the cause of their sanctification. This appears from 1 John i. 3, 7,

"That which we have seen and heard, declare we unto you, that ye also may have fellowship with us: and truly our fellowship is with the Father, and with his Son Jesus Christ. But if we walk in the light, as he is in the light, we have fellowship one with another, and the blood of Jesus Christ his Son cleanseth us from all sin."

5. *Lastly*, Unholy sinners are miserable in the want of part with Christ. They are "without Christ, being aliens from the commonwealth of Israel, and strangers from the covenants of promise, having no hope, and without God in the world," Eph. ii. 12. Therefore this struck Peter, when he saw how deep it drew: for he said, Acts iv. 12, "Neither is there salvation in any other: for there is none other name under heaven given among men whereby we must be saved." It is true, all that hear the gospel are externally called to the fellowship of his Son: but most men love the fellowship of the world lying in wickedness, and will not take part with Christ. So they are without it, though it lies open to them: and to each one of them may be said what Peter said to Simon Magus, Acts viii. 21, "Thou hast neither part nor lot in this matter: for thy heart is not right in the sight of God." Meanwhile their unholiness is not the thing that bars them from having part with Christ; but their want of part with Christ is that whereby they keep themselves unholy.

Secondly, I shall show wherein the unwashed sinner's having no part with Christ does lie or consist. This will appear, with the misery of the case, in taking a view, 1. Of Christ's work; and, 2. Of his reward; in neither of which the unholy have part with him.

First, Christ is happy, in that he has done out the work he undertook for the salvation of sinners: and all that are his have part with him therein; it is imputed to them, as if they had done it, Gal. ii. 20. And,

1. He has been born holy, and answered the demand of the law for holiness of nature, by his bringing a holy human nature into the world with him, as a public person. Hence in Luke i. 35, he is called "that holy thing born." Heb. vii. 26, "For such an high priest became us, who is holy, harmless, undefiled, separated from sinners." So that demand of the law for salvation for all that are his, is answered; for in Col. ii. 10, 11, they are said to be complete in him; and to be circumsised in him. The law cannot stop their salvation for want of a perfectly holy nature; for they have part with him, in the holiness of his nature, and that holy nature is communicated to them.[*]

---

[*] See View of the Covenant of Grace from the sacred records, head 3, concerning the conditionary part of the covenant.

But unholy sinners have no part with Christ in this matter: the holiness of Christ's nature is not imputed to them, or reckoned theirs. There is a holy birth of the second Adam, to take away the guilt of sin that we are born in: but such as are not washed by Christ from their sin, have no share in it.

The evidence of this is, that whosoever have part in the holiness of Christ's birth by imputation, are really born again in their own persons: because Christ's holy birth is the efficient meritorious cause of the new birth of his members. Hence the apostle saith, 2 Cor. v. 17, "If any man be in Christ, he is a new creature: old things are passed away, behold, all things are become new." Col. ii. 11, "In whom also ye are circumcised with the circumcision made without hands, in putting off the body of the sins of the flesh, by the circumcision of Christ." Now, the unholy are not born again; therefore they have no part with Christ in his holy birth: and so they have nothing to answer the law's demand for holiness of nature.

2. Christ has lived a righteous life, in perfect obedience to the law's commands: Philip. ii. 8, "He became obedient unto death." He did it as a public person: and all his have part with him in it; they obeyed in Christ, as they sinned in Adam, Rom. viii. 3, 4, "For what the law could not do, in that it was weak through the flesh, God sending his own Son in the likeness of sinful flesh, and for sin condemned sin in the flesh; that the righteousness of the law might be fulfilled in us, who walk not after the flesh, but after the Spirit." Hence are these epithets of the church, undefiled, without spot, complete in him. So the law's demand of obedience, as the condition of life, is answered as to them: their part in Christ's obedience answers it fully.†

But the unholy have no part with Christ in the obedience of his life. For Christ's obedience being meritorious of our sanctification, the want of the latter is a plain evidence of no part in the former; and that upon the ground of justice, which requires the delivering of the thing purchased, upon the application of the price, Rom. viii. 1,—4. If ye have obeyed legally in Christ, ye obey really in your own persons; for Christ's obedience hath a conforming virtue in those to whom it is imputed, Rom. viii. 29, "For whom he did foreknow, he also did predestinate to be conformed to the image of his Son." 1 John ii. 6, "He that saith he abideth in him, ought himself also so to walk, even as he walked." Inherent righteousness necessarily follows imputed righteousness. An unholy life argues no part in the holiness of Christ's life: therefore there is a bar between heaven and the unholy.

† See View of the Covenant of Grace, Head 3, *ut supra*.

3. He has suffered, to the full satisfaction of the law in its threatening and curse for sin, Philip. ii. 8, "He humbled himself, and became obedient unto death, even the death of the cross. Gal. iii. 13, "Christ hath redeemed us from the curse of the law, being made a curse for us: for it is written, Cursed is every one that hangeth on a tree." And Christ suffering as a public person, all that are his suffered in him, having part with him in his sufferings. They were legally crucified with him, Gal. ii. 20, died with him, Rom. vi. 10, 11, and were buried with him, Col. ii. 12. So the law's demand of satisfaction is answered for them, since they have part with Christ.*

But the unholy have no part with Christ in his sufferings. An undeniable evidence whereof is their not being conformed to him in his death, Philip. iii 10. The death of Christ will infallibly prove the death of sin, when one has part with Christ in it; Rom. vi. 6, "Knowing this, that our old man is crucified with him, that the body of sin might be destroyed, that henceforth we should not serve sin." Gal. v. 24, "They that are Christ's, have crucified the flesh, with the affections and lusts." As sure as Christ died for the sins of the elect, they will die to sin that have communion with him in it: for as death made its way from the members to the head, till it laid him in the grave; so the merit of his death will make its way from the head to them to their sanctification. So that demand of the law lies on their heads unanswered.

4. He has brought in everlasting righteousness. In what he was, did, and suffered, he fully satisfied what the law had to demand, coming up, as a public person, to an exact conformity thereto. This is the righteousness he has wrought, sufficient to cover every sinner in the sight of God, and to render him accepted as righteous. All that are his have part with him in it, Psal. xlv. 13; Cant. vi. 10; Rev. iii. 18. So they that have a righteousness that is law-biding.

But the unholy have no part with him in it. For wherever righteousness imputed is on any man, inherent holiness is in him. By the former satisfying the law, the strength of sin is taken away: so that the man cannot be living in sin as formerly. Hence the apostle saith, Rom. vi. 2, "How shall we that are dead to sin, live any longer therein?"

Secondly, Christ has received the reward of his work; and so he has an inexhaustible treasure; and all that are his have part with him in it.

1. Christ is risen again from the dead. By the authority of the

---

* See View of the Covenant of Grace, head 3, *ut supra*.

Father he is discharged from the grave; death is never to seize him more: Acts ii. 24, "God raised him up, having loosed the pains of death: because it was not possible that he should be holden of it." And all his have part with him in his ressurrection: Eph. ii. 6, "God hath raised us up together, and made us sit together in heavenly places in Christ Jesus: forasmuch as he rose as a public person. But the unholy have no part with him in his resurrection. For,

1*st*, They are still dead in their sins, while they live in them. Where is there part then in Christ's resurrection? They that have part with him are risen with him, risen by virtue of his resurrection; the power of the resurrection of the head raising the members from death in sin, Col. ii. 12; and iii. 1. Alas! the grave-clothes of the sins of the flesh, which ye are not putting off, but keeping on, and the ties whereof are still as fast upon you as ever, speak you destitute of any part with Christ in this matter.

2*dly*, They are still members of the congregation of the dead, Eph. ii. 1, 2, 3. When our Lord rose, he left the congregation of the dead in their graves; yea, he conversed not with the world thereafter, as before his death. And so, whenever a soul gets part with Christ, it leaves the world lying in wickedness, comes out from among them, and walks no more according to the course of this world. Hence the apostle saith, Rom. vi. 4, 5, "We are buried with him by baptism into death: that like as Christ was raised up from the dead by the glory of the Father, even so we also should walk in newness of life. For if we have been planted together in the likeness of his death; we shall be also in the likeness of his resurrection." What shadow of ground have they then to pretend to a part with him, that are not walking in newness of life, but just according to the course of the world.

2. Christ is now ascended up into glory, where he sits at the Father's right hand, Mark xvi. 19. He ascended into it, as a public person, to take possession of it for us, Heb. vi. 20. And all his have part with him in it, as the members of the glory of the head: Eph. ii. 6, "God hath raised us up together, and made us sit together in heavenly places in Christ Jesus."

But the unholy have no part with him in it. For,

1*st*, They are yet lying in the filth of their natural state, through original and actual sin, Psal. xiv. 3; all over defiled, Tit. i. 15. They may have worldly glory, outside glory, such as ariseth from bravery, wealth, and honour; yea they may glory in wickedness, that is really their shame. But there is no heavenly glory or any, but by sanctifying grace, 2 Cor. iii. 18; that only makes a glorious inside, Psal. xlv. 13; in so far as thereby the purity of the divine image is on the soul.

2*dly*, Neither is their heart there, nor are they making forward to it. Our Lord tells us, Matth. vi. 21, that "where the treasure is, there will the heart be also." And therefore the apostle urges, Col. iii. 1, 2, to "seek those things which are above, where Christ sitteth on the right hand of God; to set our affection on things above, not on things on the earth." What part then have they with Christ in his glory, whose affections are not on things above, but on the earth, Phil. iii. 19, "who mind earthly things?" They carry themselves as natives of the world, not as pilgrims in it. Their great aim is, to compass designs of worldly profits and pleasures, but not to be fitted for glory, 1 John iii. 3.

3. Christ has the Spirit of life and holiness dwelling in him, as the head of his body mystical. So the Spirit of life is in him, to be communicated; and it is the purchase of his death, Rev. iii. 1, "He hath the seven Spirits; seven Spirits answerable to the seven golden candlesticks; enough to quicken and actuate them all. Hence he is said to quicken, John v. 21, 26. And all his have part with him therein, Philip. ii. 1. The same Spirit that is in the head, is in the members too, in so much that "the Spirit of God dwells in them; and if any man have not the Spirit of Christ he is none of his."

But the unholy have no part with him in his Spirit For,

1*st*, He is the holy Spirit, "the Spirit of holiness," Rom. i. 4; so called not only from the work of sanctification ascribed peculiarly to him, but from the holiness of his nature, in opposition to the unclean spirit, Mark iii. 29, 30, to attest all the works of God without himself, whereof he is the immediate worker, to be holy. So that in whomsoever he dwells, and actuates, they must needs be made holy: Rom. viii. 2, "For the law of the Spirit of life, in Christ Jesus, hath made them free from the law of sin and death." Since then the unholy are under the law of sin as the subjects thereof, and under the law of spiritual death, they have no part with Christ.

2*dly*, They have the spirit of the world in them, conforming them to the world, in their frame of heart, way, and walk, 1 John iv. 4. It is an unclean, unholy spirit, whereby they cannot relish nor favour the holy things of God: but things that are fleshy, sensual, carnal, and earthly, Jude ver. 19; not without a secret enmity at true holiness, Rom. viii. 7, and cannot hold on in the way of God, as Caleb did, Num. xiv. 24.

3*dly*, They live in the state wherein Adam left them, without a saving change. 1 Cor. xv. 45, Adam was made "a living soul," but Christ "a quickening spirit." What men derive from Adam, they have; a natural life, a life of reason, gifts of knowledge, &c. But what men derive from Christ, they have not; they are not quickened by him with the Spirit of life unto God. But if they had part with Christ, they would be spiritually quickened souls; as sure as having part with Adam, they are living souls.

4. There is a fulness of grace in the man Christ: Col. i. 19, "For it pleased the Father, that in him should all fulness dwell." John i. 14, "The Word was full of grace and truth." Grace is given him without measure, John iii. 4; and all that are his partake with him in it, it being in him as in the storehouse; it is so poured on him as the head, that it runs down to the skirts of his garment, John i. 16.

But the unholy have no part with him in his grace. For,

1*st*, They are not partakers of the divine nature, that new nature which is derived from Christ, by the communication of grace from him by the Spirit into his mystical members, whereby they escape the corruption of the world, 2 Pet. i. 4. Instead of that, the old nature reigns in them, which is enmity against God, and serious religion. The old man with his deeds is still in his vigour, has not yet got his deadly wound.

2*dly*, Whatever good or grace may seem to be in them, it is but in some one or few particulars. There are still several black buts in their religion; they never make thorough work of it, Psal. cxix. 6, They have not respect unto all God's commandments. For they are never made new creatures; though some things, yet never are all things become new with them. An evidence that they have no part in the grace of Christ; for then should they have grace for grace.

3*dly*, Hence they do not bear Christ's image: they are not like him, in the set of their spirit, and tenor of their walk: 1 John ii. 6, "For he that saith he abideth in him, ought himself also so to walk, even as he walked." They look like the old Adam, sinful, sensual, and averse from God. But O how unlike the holy crucified Jesus, and how quite unconcerned to be like him, their own consciences bear witness. But the having part with Christ makes a person like him.

5 *Lastly*, Christ is anointed of the Father with the Spirit to be the Prophet, Priest, and King of his church. Hence he says himself, Is. lxi. 1. "The spirit of the Lord God is upon me, because the Lord hath anointed me to preach good tidings unto the meek, he hath sent me to bind up the broken-hearted, to proclaim liberty to the captive, and the opening of the prison to them that are bound." And the apostle Peter saith, Acts x. 38, that "God anointed Jesus of Nazareth with the Holy Ghost, and with power; who went

about doing good, and healing all that were oppressed of the devil: for God was with him." This is the honour put on him, to bear these offices, signified by his names Messias and Christ, *i. e.* anointed. And as he is Christ, all that are his are Christians, anointed with the same Spirit, Psal. xlv. 7, having part with him in his offices.

1*st*, Christ is a prophet: and all that are his, have part with him in his prophetical office, are prophets too, Psal. cv. 15. They are let into the knowledge of the things of God by the Spirit. Hence the apostle saith, 1 John ii. 20, 27, "But ye have an unction from the Holy One, and ye know all things. But the anointing which ye have received of him, abideth in you: and ye need not that any man teach you: But, as the same anointing teacheth you of all things, and is truth and is no lie: and even as it hath taught you, ye shall abide in him." They are on the secret of heaven: For (Psal. xxv. 14,) "the secret of the Lord is with them that fear him: and he will shew them his covenant," Matt. xi. 25. And they teach them to others too, though they cannot make them effectual. Hence David saith, Psal. li. 13, "I will teach transgressors thy ways, and sinners shall be converted unto thee." Not only ministers, but every true Christian has this office; the former in a public, the latter in a private captivity, Philip. ii. 15, 16.

But the unholy have no part with him in his prophetical office.

(1.) They are not illuminated by the Spirit of holiness, savingly to know the things of God, 1 Cor. ii. 12, 14. They may be taught by men, but are not taught of God: they may know the literal sense of the words of the gospel; but the things thereof in their suitableness to the divine perfections and sinner's case, are are hid from them, Matt. xi. 25. They never get into the secret of religion.

(2.) Neither do they by the Spirit of holiness enlighten the world. Being dark themselves, they darken the world by their ungodly, profane, or formal lives. Most of them see no tie on them to be their brother's keeper. Such as teach others the things of God, do it by a gift, for their own glory; not by the Spirit, out of love to Christ and his glory. So they have no part with him in his prophetical office.

2*dly*, He is a Priest: and all his have part with him in that venerable office. They are priests too, 1 Pet. ii. 9, a royal priesthood: Rev. i. 6, priests unto God. They are consecrated to God to serve him in his spiritual temple, in their robes of Christ's imputed righteousness and inherent holiness. They offer sacrifices of thanksgiving unto God, which are accepted of God through Christ, their only altar.

They offer to him themselves, Rom. xii. 1, their service to him in acts of worship and duty, Heb. xiii. 15; Acts x. 4, and in suffering or bearing the cross, Philip. ii. 17; 2 Tim. iv. 6.

But the unholy have no part with Christ in his priestly office.

(1.) They are not of the line, not descended from our great High Priest, as born of his Spirit. They were never truly consecrated, or made holy persons; they are destitute of imputed and implanted righteousness: they are wholly polluted and defiled, as being of the world lying in wickedness: so if they pretend to the spiritual priesthood, they will be, as polluted, put from it.

(2.) They do not, nor cannot offer acceptable sacrifices to God. They never offer themselves to God as a sacrifice, but to the world and their lusts. If they offer prayers or other services to him, they never offer them on the right altar, Christ. Hence they, and all they do, even their best things, are an abomination, Prov. xxviii. 9.

Lastly, Christ is a King: and all his have part with him in that honourable office. They are kings too, Rev. i. 6, "Kings unto God." They have the right of dominion over their spiritual enemies, the rule of their own spirits governing themselves by the laws of Christ, and the lordship of the world, Rom. iv. 13; and they are heirs of the kingdom of heaven. They do not yet peaceably possess their kingdom; the rebels and their open enemies are making constant wars against them; but they do overcome, and are "more than conquerors, through him that loved them," 1 John iv. 4; Rom. viii. 37.

But the unholy have no part with Christ in his kingly office.

They are servants and slaves to sin and Satan, Rom. vi. 16. They are under the power of Satan, Acts xxvi. 18; led captive at his will, 2 Tim. ii. 26. They have no gracious management of their own spirits, Prov. xxv. 28. They are the servants of corruption; they can neither think nor do any service acceptable to God.

THE APPLICATION.

I shut up all with some practical inferences.

INFERENCE 1. Holiness is absolutely necessary to happiness: for (Heb. xii. 14,) "without holiness no man shall see the Lord." Ye may be either poor or rich, sick or whole, and yet be happy. But if ye be not holy, ye are miserable; for ye have no part with Christ, And, Acts iv. 12, "There is no salvation in any other: for there is none other name under heaven given among men whereby we must be saved." It is astonishing to think, how easy many that hear the gospel are about holiness; they are in no concern whether they be holy or not. They would not have people to take them for saints;

nay, holy people are a jest with them. There is no accounting for this any other way but that holiness is rare in the world, and they have no mind to be singular, nor to distinguish themselves from "the world lying in wickedness."

But consider these four things.

1. God is holy. The God that made you is holy by necessity of nature; he is so holy that he cannot be but holy. If God is necessarily holy, he cannot but hate unholiness; because he cannot but love his own image, and hate what is contrary to his nature: therefore he cannot but hate your unholiness, and for it hate you who are unholy. And what we hate as contrary to our nature, we seek to destroy. Now, consider the misery of being objects of God's hatred and aversion, and what makes you so; and ye will see the necessity of your being holy, 1 Pet. i. 16, "Be ye holy," saith the Lord, "for I am holy."

2. Christ our Saviour is holy. As he is God, he is "the holy One of Israel;" as he is man, he is "that holy thing," Luke i. 35. Jesus is called "the holy One;" the very devils owned him to be so, Mark i. 24. The very end of his being Jesus, was to make men holy, Matth. i. 21, "Thou shalt call his name Jesus: for he shall save his people from their sins." He came to destroy the works of the devil, he died to redeem sinners from their sins, Tit. ii. 14. What part then can ye possibly imagine yourselves to have in him, while ye continue unholy?

3. The body of Christ is holy; they that belong to him, the company of the saved, Eph. v. 25, 26. The devil is the god of this world; his subjects are the world lying in wickedness. Out of them Christ raises his kingdom, and his subjects are all holy, Gal. iv. 4; Rev. xix. 14. It is their distinguishing badge from those that belong to Satan, that agrees to them all, and to them only, 2 Tim. ii. 19. So that if ye are not holy, ye belong not to Christ, but to Satan.

4. Heaven is holy; it is a holy state, a holy place, where no unholy thing can enter, Rev. xxi. 27. As to the dogs and swine, their place will be without, Rev. xxi. 15, that is, the unholy, who "go with the dog to the vomit, and with the sow that was washed to the wallowing in the mire," shall be cast out from the supper of the saints in glory into outer darkness, Matth. viii. 12.

INFERENCE 2. There is no true holiness, but in communion with Christ. Men may have a shew and semblance of holiness, without union and communion with Christ. But real holiness acceptable to God, no man attains but in Christ, being sanctified only with his blood, by his Spirit, through faith; made new creatures after his image, by participation of the all-fulness of grace in him, as at large declared, 1 Cor. i. 2; Eph. ii. 10; 1 Pet. i. 2; Acts xxvi. 18.

And therefore holiness is quite another thing, than,

1. Common civility. A man may be civil, not rude, but courteous, discreet, and obliging in his conversation; and yet be a stranger to holiness. This was the case of the young man, of whom, "when Jesus saw that he answered discreetly, he said unto him, Thou art not far from the kingdom of God," Mark xii. 34. There are some rude persons that bear the devil's mark on their foreheads, who behave themselves neither according to the rules of grace nor good manners: some professors that affect and pride themselves in rudeness, regarding no body, nor their offence, but only to please themselves. Such would do well to consider, whether that be consistent with real holiness or not. The reason of the doubt, is the second great command of the law, "Thou shalt love thy neighbour as thyself." Howbeit, civility is not holiness, though a part of the matter of it.

2. Morality, whether we understand by it common honesty in dealings in the world; or a conformity to the letter of the law, which makes a blameless outward conversation, and goes under the name of moral virtue, but has no relation to Christ and his Spirit. Men may have all this, and not be holy; as had the Pharisee, Luke xviii. 11, who "stood and prayed thus with himself, God, I thank thee, that I am not as other men are, extortioners, unjust, adulterers, or even as this publican." This was also the case of Paul, Phil. iii. 6, "Concerning zeal, persecuting the church; touching the righteousness which is in the law, blameless." These fruits are in many like the apples of Sodom, which are fair to look at, but when handled fall to ashes.

3. A form of godliness, 2 Tim. iii. 5. There may be the going the round of the external duties of religion, where there is no holiness: for these may be done by them that are without Christ, Luke xviii. 12; Matt. v. 20; Is. lviii. 2, 3; though many place all their religion in these things, as if they pray, communicate, &c. to be concerned no more to be holy.

All these differ from true holiness,

1*st*, In the original and spring of them. True holiness springs from union with Christ, the Spirit applying the blood of Christ to the soul, received by faith, improving the word, sacraments, and afflictions. The Spirit is the efficient cause, the blood the meritorious cause, and faith the instrumental cause of true sanctification. But these others have a far lower rise. They are the effect of good education and breeding; of unsanctified consideration of their own circumstances and worldly interest, that oblige many to take up themselves, and live regularly; of fear and hope; of respect to credit and reputation; and in some, of legal convictions.

2dly, In the subject of them. Holiness diffuseth itself through the whole man, inward and outward, 2 Cor. v. 17; 1 Thess. v. 23. These are mere plasterings of the outward man, while enmity against God, rancour against serious godliness, and reigning power of lusts in the heart, do remain in their native force, and the old man bears full sway within; as appears in the Pharisees. They make a new life, but they leave the old nature unhealed, unrenewed.

3dly, In the extent of them. True holiness extends to all the Lord commands and forbids, Psal. cxix. 6; for the whole law is written in the heart, Heb. viii. 10; and so they are holy in all manner of conversation. These never take in more than some shreds of the law; such men never set themselves to conform to it in its spirituality. They quite neglect many of the duties thereof; they consider them not, or they contemn them: for they have no mind to take more of them, than makes for their purpose.

Lastly, In the nature and kind of them. True holiness is a cluster of the fruits of the Spirit, Gal. v. 22, "Love, joy, peace, long-suffering, gentleness, goodness, faith, meekness, temperance." They are acts of moral discipline, which have self-love in an unrenewed heart, not the love of God in a renewed heart, for their principle. The reason of them is not the will of God; for reasons of their own they do so, but not because God commands it. They do not their works in faith of the promise of assistance from heaven, nor of acceptance for Christ's sake; but out of their own stock, little valuing whether they be accepted or no; or if they do, looking for acceptance on their intrinsic worth. Their end is not the glory of God, and to express their gratitude; but as they come from self, so they are swallowed up in self.

INFERENCE 3. Vain are the pretences of the unholy to part with Christ; for no unwashed sinner has part with the holy Jesus. They do but deceive themselves in their pretending thereto; and the deceit will out on them to their eternal confusion, if they see it not timely. Here consider,

1. Who are unwashed sinners; and,
2. The state of unwashed sinners, as having no part with Christ.
1. Consider who are unwashed sinners. In the general,

1st, Those who have not yet escaped the pollutions of the world in the outward man, but in the course of their lives are conform to the world lying in wickedness, Psal. xxiv. 3, 4; Gal. v. 19—21.

How can they pretend to be washed, on whom the gross filth of sin is still lying visible in their outward life and conversation? Men may escape that, and yet not be truly washed; escape and yet be intangled again by apostacy. Let none such pretend to have part in Christ, 2 Pet. ii. 20, 21, for Christ will disown them.

2*dly*, They that have no apparent beauty of holiness on them, 1 Thess. v. 5. Men deceive themselves in despising the appearance of holiness, scorning to appear holy. That is but a peace of fashionable contempt of religion, poured on it in compliance to an ungodly world, and a naughty heart: for wherever grace is in the heart, it will shine forth in the life, Matth. vi. 22; Philip. ii. 15, 16. And though men may appear holy, who are not so; yet no man can be holy that has no appearance of it. If there is any religion at at all in the world, it must be among them that have an appearance of it, and not among those that have not.

More particularly, they are yet unwashed by Christ,

1*st*, Who have never yet had the glass of the law held to their face, in a work of conviction of the sinfulness of their nature, heart, and life, John xvi. 8. Christ washes none till he has discovered to them their pollution. For till then they will never see their need of washing. He washeth by the word, as by its light it convinceth of defilement, points out the cleanness to be aimed at, and sets the soul astir anxiously to seek it.

2*dly*, Who have not yet got a view of the filthiness, loathsomeness, and abominable nature of sin, Ezek. xxxvi. 31. Men's consciences may be fired with a sense of the guilt of sin; so as they may be brought to cast it out as a coal that would burn them; that yet are blind to the filth of sin, and see not how it defiles them. This appears, in that if they could be but safe from wrath, they would never part with sin.

3*dly*, Who have not yet been made willing to be made clean. None are washed against their will, Jer. xiii. 27. And there is need of a day of power to make willing, Psal. cx. 3. Men naturally love to be still in the pollution of their sin, as the sow to wallow in the mire. They are as loath to be brought away, as fishes to come out of the water. Nay, there is in every unregenerate man, a heart enmity against holiness, Rom. viii. 7. The heart spits its venom against it. They are not only not fond of it, but they hate it: A certain indication, that they are void of it.

4*thly*, Who have never yet felt an absolute need of Christ, his blood and Spirit, for their sanctification; and so have not yet come to Christ by faith for it, Hos. v. 13; Psal. li. 2; and lxv. 3. There is no washing but by Christ, and in union with him: therefore they who have not come to Christ for sanctification, whatever pains they have been at to wash themselves, are yet unwashed.

2. Consider the state of unwashed sinners as having no part with Christ. Having no part with Christ,

1*st*, They have no part in the favour of God, Eph. ii. 12. They are " without Christ, being aliens from the commonwealth of Israel, and strangers from the covenants of promise, having no hope, and without God in the world." They are yet in a state of enmity with God; for he only is our peace, and the only way to the Father. All their sins, original and actual, in the guilt of them, do yet lie upon them: there is not one *item* blotted out of their account. For God gives no pardons, but to sinners in Christ: they must meet him there who would be pardoned or reconciled, 3 Cor. v. 19.

2*dly*, They are loathsome in God's sight; his soul abhors them as abominable, Tit. i. 15. No sinner can be savoury in God's sight, but by the sweet-smelling savour of Christ's sacrifice upon them. The smell of Jacob was sweet to Isaac, in the goodly raiment of his elder brother: and sinners are savoury to God, only in Christ, 2 Cor. ii. 15. While the sinner has no part with Christ, the filth of all his sin, original and actual, lies on him; and there is nothing on him to master the filthy savour arising therefrom.

3*dly*, They have no part with the family of God, but with " the world lying in wickedness, 1 John i. 3, and v. 19, " They are aliens from the commonwealth of Israel, and strangers from the covenants of promise, having no hope, and without God in the world," being without Christ, Eph. ii. 12. They have no right to the privileges of God's children; for none can have that but in the right of Christ as his head. What is the state of the world lying in wickedness, is their state. They are under God's wrath, and the curse of the law.

Lastly, They shall have no part with the saints in light, but their part will be with sinners in outer darkness, Col. i. 12, 13; Rev. xxii. 15. One who has no part with Christ here, will have no part in heaven hereafter for none can come there, but in and through him. They will have their part in "the lake which burneth with fire and brimstone," Rev. xxi. 8.

INFERENCE 4, *Lastly*, The way to be washed from sin, and made holy, is to get part with Christ by faith.

1. Think not that ye must first be holy, before ye can have part with Christ: but ye must first have that part with Christ, ere ye can be holy, as appears from what is said. The former is as absurd as to say, the sick must be cured ere he come to the physician, and the filthy washed ere he come to the waters. Hence, (1.) Your unholiness cannot bar you from getting part with Christ. (2.) The first step to holiness is to believe.

2. This is a sure way to holiness; it cannot misgive. For hereby the sick are put in the hand of the physician, the filthy in the laver. The sinner united to Christ, must needs partake of his blood and Spirit: as through our relation to Adam we are defiled, so by our relation to Christ we come to be sanctified.

3. *Lastly,* This is the only way, as being of God's appointment. The sanctification of a sinner is above the power of nature, not to be reached by natural endeavours; they have not that word of appointment.

THE CHRISTIAN WARFARE; OR, THE GOOD FIGHT OF FAITH.

Several Sermons, preached at Ettrick, in the year 1723,

1 Timothy vi. 12,

Fight the good fight of faith.

The Apostle having given Timothy an exhortation to several particular duties, here gives him an exhortation to the Christian life in general. Wherein we have two things.

1. A description of the Christian life. It is not an easy, idle, inactive life; but, (1.) A fight, a combat, a wrestling: for there are many enemies set to keep us out of the promised land. (2.) A good fight. There are many ill fights in the world. The men of the world have many fights and squabbles about this world, the honours, advantages, and pleasures of it, not worth the fighting for. But it is a good fight, a noble and worthy fight, wherein true valour and magnanimity appears. (3.) A fight of faith. Some understand this of the doctrine of faith, as that which is to be fought for. I understand it rather of the grace of faith, by which the fight is to be managed. This comprehends the former; and is more agreeable to the practical directions, ver. 11, and the "laying hold on eternal life," which is done by the grace of faith. So it is a fight to be managed in the way of believing.

2. The word of command given: "Fight the good fight of faith:" Agonize, like a combatant, wrestler, puting forth your utmost vigour. Timothy was engaged already in the fight; but still he was in the field of battle, and the enemy not yet off the field: therefore it is said to him, Fight. Paul was going off the field, and he says, "I have fought a good fight, I have finished my course, I have

kept the faith," 2 Tim. iv. 7. Timothy was come on the field, and to him it was said, Fight.

The doctrine natively arising from the words, is this.

DOCTRINE. The Christian life is the good fight of faith, that must be fought by all that would see heaven.

In discoursing this doctrine, we shall shew,

I. In what respects the Christian life is the fight of faith.

II. In what respects it is a good fight.

III. Why the Christian life in the disposal of holy providence, is made a fight.

IV. Why a fight of faith.

V. Touch at some particular fights of faith the Christian may have in his course heavenward.

I. We shall shew in what respects the Christian life is the fight of faith. I take up this in these seven things.

1. There are enemies of our salvation, and there must be faith in the soul to set against them. Where there are not two parties, there can be no fight. There is no fighting in heaven, for there are no enemies there, Rev. xxi. 25. There is none of this fighting in the unbelieving world neither; for the enemies have all there alone, and there is no faith to set against them, Luke xi. 21. Unbelief carries the man quite over to the enemy's side; it is the evil spy, that says, It is needless to think on the fight. This fight is only found where faith and its opposites meet; and that is in the Christian's heart and life: Cant. vi. ult. "What will ye see in the Shulamite? as it were the company of two armies." So the combatant is only the man that has given up his name to Christ, and listed with him.

2. The enemy will not be quiet; he will make an attack on the believer setting heavenward. Hence is that exhortation, 1. Pet. v. 8, "Be sober, be viligant; because your adversary the devil, as a roaring lion, walketh about seeking whom he may devour." Satan may rock his own children, and labour to keep all quiet: the more secure they lie, they are in the less hazard to break away from him. But God's children must not look for such treatment: their faces are away-ward from his kingdom; and therefore the enemy's face will be set against them, as a prize.

3. God's people must resist: 1 Pet. v. 9, "Whom [Satan] resist stedfast in the faith." They must set themselves to stand their ground against all opposition, and grapple with the difficulties in their way to heaven, Luke xiii. 24. They must be denied to their ease, content to quit their soft beds of ease, and take the field for it, and endure hardness, 2 Tim ii. 3.

4. They must resist by faith, 1 Pet. v. 9. above-cited. Faith is the mouth of the soul, that must give the shout in this battle, the hands the men of might must find in it, the weapon they must wield in it, both in the offensive and defensive part of it: Eph. vi. 16, "Above all, taking the shield of faith, wherewith ye shall be able to quench all the fiery darts of the wicked." So one must not only have the grace of faith, but he must have it in exercise.

5. They must continue in that resistance, and hold on in it: Eph. vi. 13, "Take unto you the whole armour of God, that ye may be able to withstand in the evil day, and having done all to stand." The Christian life is a fight, and that denotes a continuance. Many think they should have no more ado, but whenever an enemy starts up, to lay at him with a stroke, and strike him down; and so be easy again: and so they perplex themselves with doubts, fears, and jealousies of the love of God, because it is otherwise with them, the enemy being still fresh and vigorous, Is. xxvi. 18. But alas! Sirs, ye should consider, that that may be striking indeed, but not a fight, being of no continuance.

6. They must lay their account with ups and downs, getting as well as giving wounds in the encounter. Hence says David, Psal. xxx. 7, "Lord, by thy favour thou hast made my mountain to stand strong: thou didst hide thy face, and I was troubled." Prevailing Jacob halted in his thigh, after his struggle of faith with the angel. To be absolute masters over the enemy, would not be the fight of faith, but the triumph of faith, which is reserved for heaven. In the fight of faith, the Christian may be set to his knees, but must not give over: yea, though the enemy should lay him on his back, he must say, "Rejoice not against me, O mine enemy: when I fall, I shall arise; when I sit in darkness, the Lord shall be a light unto me," Mic. vii. 8, and so bend to his feet again.

7. *Lastly*, Faith has the chief interest in this fight. In it there will be use for all the graces, the doing and suffering graces: yet the fight has its name from faith, as that which has the chief hand in it. For,

1*st*, It is faith's possession that the plea is about. Life and salvation in Christ Jesus is held forth, offered, and exhibited in the gospel to the sinner; and the sinner believing in Christ, appropriates and takes possession of it by faith: Cant. ii. 16, "My beloved is mine, and I am his." John xx. 28, "Thomas answered and said unto him, My Lord and my God." 1 John v. 11, 12, "This is the record, that God hath given to us eternal life; and this life is in his Son. He that hath the Son, hath life; and he that hath not the Son of God, hath not life." There is the ground of the quarrel the enemy has. If the man will quit his plea for life and salvation by Christ, the fight is at an end; the enemy has his design. But if not, the alarm is sounded, and the fight begins to force him from it.

2dly, It is faith that holds fast the possession which the enemy would force from the man. For it is the bond of union betwixt Christ and the soul, and it is that which is the hold of Christ and eternal life : Heb. x. 35, 38, "Cast not away therefore your confidence, which hath great recompense of reward. Now the just shall live by faith." Therefore, believing, we are said to cleave to the Lord, to hold fast what we have, &c. The securities and rights to the heavenly inheritance are the promises; faith gripes them, and so keeps possession.

3dly, It is faith that, of all the graces, is the main actor in this fight. Those worthies in Heb. xi. exercised and had need of all the graces of the Spirit. There was much love, humility, meekness, patience, &c. in their doing and suffering so great things: but all is ascribed to faith. For faith is the captain of all the graces; it leads them out, puts an edge upon them for the fight, and makes them active. And therefore, in this fight, the word that is given from heaven, is, "Be not afraid, only believe," Mark v. 36, "Above all, taking the shield of faith, wherewith ye shall be able to quench all the fiery darts of the wicked," Eph. vi. 16.

QUESTION. How comes it that faith has the preference among all the rest of the graces in this fight? ANSWER. On these accounts,

(1.) It is the grace that is first on the field of battle, and all the rest follow it. It is the first link of the chain of the graces of the Spirit, that draws all the rest after it, 1 Tim. i. 5. It is the mother-grace, out of whose womb they all come forth; because it is the uniting grace that knits the soul to Christ, the fountain of fulness. So the way to get love, repentance, patience, &c. is to believe, thus it furnishes the field of battle, with fighters on Christ's side.

(2.) It strengthens them all, according to its measure; for that is the rule of the dispensation of grace, "According to thy faith, be it unto thee." According as it is weak or strong, so are they: for it is not only the mother-grace but the nursing grace. Faith lies as it were nearest the fountain, and is the channel of conveyance of supply: so as it gets in, they get out for their nourishment.

(3.) It brings the healing they get to their wounds. Many a time the Christian's love is foundered in this fight, and is like to bleed to death, by an arrow of jealousy of God shot into their breast. Faith gives the combatant a sight of the glory of God in the face of Jesus; and so pulls out the arrow, John ii. 4. Their patience is wounded, that it can no longer stand; faith brings the promise, Heb. ii. 3, "For the vision is yet for an appointed time, but at the end it shall speak, and not lie: though it tarry, wait for it, because it will surely come, it will not tarry," and it sets patience to its feet again. It brings the leaves of the tree of life, applies them to the wounds, and heals them; so the fight is renewed.

(4.) It carries on the fight, and obtains the victory: 2 Pet. v. 9, "Whom resist, stedfast in the faith." 1 John v. 4, "This is the victory that overcometh the world, even our faith." It is by faith the enemy is put to flight, that partial victories are obtained during this life, and that the total victory is obtained at death, 2 Tim. iv. 7, 8. Thus by faith the martyrs swimmed through a sea of blood to the other side. And hence,

4thly, The great design of the enemy is to weaken faith, and to wrest it away out of the combatants hand. It was by unbelief of the threatening of the first covenant, that Satan ruined the world at first: and now his great business is, to keep men from believing the promise of the second covenant. He knows full well their strength lies there; and take away that, they shall be as other men, that he may do with them what he will.

Lastly, The great design of a holy God, in that fight is the trial of faith. Hence says the apostle, 1 Pet. i. 6, 7, "Wherein ye greatly rejoice, though now for a season (if need be) ye are in heaviness through manifold temptations: that the trial of your faith being much more precious than of gold that perisheth, though it be tried with fire, might be found unto praise, and honour, and glory, at the appearing of Jesus Christ." Faith acts in trusting an unseen God, believing his word, living upon the credit of the promise. Thus the Lord will have his people to go through the wilderness of this world, "walking by faith, not by sight." When they come to heaven the trial of faith is over: so there is no more fight.

II. The second thing is, to shew in what respects it is a good fight.

1. The cause is good. Many fight to carry their ill cause by force, and their fightings proceed from an eager desire to satisfy their lusts, James iv. 1, 2. But here is a good fight for a good cause, cleaving to the Lord over the belly of all difficulties; laying hold, and keeping hold, of eternal life. It is the cause of God, the cause of Christ, the cause of the sinner's eternal salvation, which cannot be but a good cause, to endeavour the maintenance of against all opposers.

2. It is an honourable fight, worthy of a man of true valour and magnanimity, 1 Cor. ix. 25—27; Prov. xvi. 32. The men of the

world boast themselves of their strength in making their part good against weak worms like themselves. In the mean time they are slaves to the devil and their lusts, and have neither heart nor hand to resist them, but are captive at pleasure. But the believer in his fight encounters more formidable enemies: Eph. vi. 12, "We wrestle not against flesh and blood, but against principalities, against powers, against the rulers of the darkness of this world, against spiritual wickedness in high places."

3. There is a good captain in this fight, the Lord Jesus Christ, under whose standard the believer fights, Heb. ii. 10. He went on the head of all the fighting company and overcame; and he calls his people to make their way through an army which he has already broken: Rev. iii. 21, "To him that overcometh will I grant to sit with me in my throne, even as I also overcame, and am set down with my Father in his throne." He is ever at their hand, and the cause is his; it must therefore needs be a good fight.

4. In regard of the good that is got even of the partial victories; the believers being helped to stand shocks, and get over them, though the war be not ended. Hence says the apostle, Rom. v. 3, 4, 5, "We glory in tribulations, knowing that tribulation worketh patience; and patience, experience; and experience, hope: and hope maketh not ashamed." The sharp trials of faith are hard in the time: but a review of bypast dangers, of the Lord's working for the soul in the time of the combat, gives an exquisite pleasure: so that the man comes to say, It is good that I was afflicted.

5. *Lastly*, In regard the final and complete victory in the end, is sure. Hence says the apostle, Rom. xvi. 20, "The God of peace shall bruise Satan under your feet shortly." Many a battle the believer may lose in the course of the war; he may be shamefully foiled: but though the enemy prevail so far, yet the believer shall always be the conqueror at the end. The men of Ai got an advantage against Joshua's men: but it did not last; they got a complete victory at length over the men of Ai.

III. Why is the Christian life, in the disposal of holy providence, made a fight? No doubt the Lord could have given his people a constant sunshine as well on this side as the other side of death, and cleared the way of those armed adversaries that are ready to attack them.

1. That the members may be conformed to their head in their passage through the world. The life that our Lord Jesus had in the world, was a fighting life all along, till he left the world, and entered into his glory. It is very agreeable then, that his followers should find it so, and so be conformed to their head in suffering as well as

in reigning: Rom. viii. 17, "If so be that we suffer with him, that we may be also glorified together." 2 Tim. ii. 12, "If we suffer, we shall also reign with him,"

2. That the nothingness, and utter unworthiness of the creature, which is to wear the crown of glory for ever, may convincingly appear; so as they themselves and all others may see it is owing purely to free grace, not to them, Deut. viii. 2. We find the Lord usually laid those very low whom he minded to raise up on high; as in the case of Joseph, Moses, and David: and this to stain the pride of all glory, that they might see their own unworthiness, and that it was wholly of free grace, and owing to no merit of theirs. The Lord accordingly minding to bring a select company into heaven at length, in the first place brings them into the wilderness. There they are stung with serpents, scorched with thirst, &c. whereby much corruption and weakness appeared in them, &c. and afterwards they are brought unto a wealthy place.

3. For the greater confusion of the grand adversary, who, attacked him in person in the world, and whom he causeth poor weak creatures to triumph over after they have maintained a fight with him, Rom. xvi. 20, "The God of peace shall bruise Satan under your feet shortly." Our Lord Jesus overcame and baffled Satan's temptations in the wilderness. He triumphed over him on the cross, where the heat of the battle was: Col. ii. 15, "Having spoiled principalities and powers, he made a shew of them openly, triumphing over them in it." Satan renews the battle against his members on earth: and what is the issue? The strippling, with his sling and stone, lays Goliath on the green. The weak believer through faith confounds the united wit and force of men and devils, Luke x. 19, which tends to the greater confusion of the enemy.

4. For the greater glory of the captain of their salvation, the more full display of the freedom of grace, and the efficacy of his blood and Spirit. (1.) Every wound the believer gets in this fight, puts a new jewel in Christ's crown. For every new wound requires a new plaister from Christ. That is a new item for the believer in the debt-book of free grace, and so puts him more in free grace's debt. (2.) Every wound the believer gives in this fight, considering his weakness and fecklessness, and the strength and subtility of the enemy, does the same.

5. For that they may have a greater variety of experiences: Rom. v. 4, "Patience worketh experience; and experience, hope." The exercised Christian is the man of most experience. There is a great variety of promises in the covenant, for the various cases the children of God may be in: and that his people may have experi-

once of the relish of these promises, he brings them into the cases to which these promises are adapted. Who finds the sap of that promise, Is. xxxiii. 16, "Bread shall be given him, his waters shall be sure," like those that are put to a fight of faith for their daily bread; or of that, Deut. xxxii. 36, "For the Lord shall judge his people, and repent himself for his servants; when he seeth that their power is gone, and there is none shut up, or left, like" those whose case is brought to an extremity in point of hopelessness?

6. *Lastly*, That heaven may be the more sweet to them, when they come to it. It is in this respect that heaven is called a place of comfort, Luke xvi. 25, wiping away of tears, rest from labours. None will find rest so sweet as the wearied man. A child of God come to his journey's end, after many falls and risings, after many ups and downs; set ashore after a dangerous voyage, will sing the song of Moses and of the Lamb in a higher strain, than if he had never been in danger from his first setting out.

IV. The fourth thing is, to shew why their fight is called a fight of faith. The reason is, because by that means all the glory of the victories obtained redounds to free grace, not to the sinner himself: Rom. iv. 16, "It is of faith, that it might be by grace." The Lord is jealous of his own glory, and sinful man is very apt to ascribe something to himself; therefore faith is pitched upon; for its activity lies in these two.

1. In carrying the sinner quite out of himself, and from off his own bottom. Hence believers are said to have no confidence in the flesh, Philip. iii. 3. The unbeliever's great strength lies in summoning together all the power of his natural abilities, and in confidence thereof trying the battle. But faith makes a man to be denied to all his own abilities, and not to lean to himself, his light, strength, &c. And therefore as the fire burns keenest in the sharp frost, so faith acts most vigorously, when sentence of death is passed on all probable means, as Abraham's faith.

2. In leaning upon the Lord for all. Hence believers are also said to rejoice in Christ Jesus, Philip. iii. 3. Faith goes out to the battle in the name of the Lord, holding by his promise, trusting that he will make it out: and so it is the mouth of the soul that sucks the sap of the promise, by a fiducial application of it, and trusting in it.

V. I will touch at some particular fights of faith, the Christian may have in his course heavenward, such as,

1. In a call to some more than ordinary work or duty.

2. In desertion.

3. In temptations from Satan.
4. In afflictions.
5. With this present evil world.
6. With sin.
7. With death.

First, There is a fight of faith, in a call to some more than ordinary work or duty. Sometimes the Lord takes trial of his people by calling them to some extraordinary piece of duty. Thus Abraham was called out to this field, Gen. xxii. 1; Moses to bring the children of Israel out of Egypt, Exod. iii; and Jonah, to preach to the Ninevites.

Here the believer gets his hands full, as much as he is able to wrestle with; yea, and sometimes as much as lays him by, his faith failing. Thus Jonah was so put to it in this fight, that he goes to fly towards Tarshish, to shift the duty.

Now, what makes the difficulty here, are, (1.) The hardness of the work in itself, as in Abraham's case. (2.) A deep sense of our inability for it, as in the case of Moses, when commanded to bring the children of Israel out of Egypt, Exod. iv. 10. For sometimes it is that which the Christian seems of all things to be most unfit for. (3.) The great danger there may be in it, so that the Christian must run a risk in setting about it. Sometimes he must risk his reputation, as in Jonah's case; sometimes he must risk even his safety or life. Here there is a particular fight of faith to be fought. And therein faith is to be exerted,

1. In complying with God's call in the faith of the promise of strength for it. Hence says the apostle, Philip. iv. 13, "I can do all things through Christ which strengtheneth me." God never calls his people to any duty, but what they have ground to expect furniture for from himself in the way of believing: "No man goeth a warfare on his own charges." God's call implies a promise of furniture: "The way of the Lord is strength to the upright." And God suits the back to the burden. It is much alike then whether it be little work and little strength, or great work and strength conform.

2. In following the duty, in the faith of divine protection, as far as he sees good. Faith trusts God with one's safety in the way of duty, according to the promise, Psal. xci. 11, "He shall give his angels charge over thee, to keep thee in all thy ways." As long as one is found in the way where God bids him go, he may be sure God will set a hedge about him, and make all work together for his good.

Secondly, There is a fight of faith in desertion. Here the believer is on the dark mountains in a special manner, the Lord in the depth of sovereign wisdom withdrawing from him. And in this case there may be several things very heavy.

1. Darkness covering the believer's spirit, Is. l. 10, whereby he goes mourning without the sun. Their former light is taken away, and clouds and mists arise, so they cannot know their way.

2. Indisposition for duty, proceeding sometimes from a listlessness to communion with God, Cant. v. 2, sometimes from the extremity of trouble, Psal. lxxvii. 4. So that the soul is not more unfit for duty, than when there is most need.

3. An army of doubts and fears attacking them, doubting of their love to God, and God's love to them, Psal. lxxvii. 7, downwards.

4. The terrors of God set in battle-array against them, Job. vi. 4. They "remember God, and are troubled," Psal. lxxvii. 3, The man is carried captive from Sion to Sinai ; the discharge is lost, and the law bends up a process against him. God appears an enemy, Psal. lxxxviii. 15.

Now faith's part here in this fight is,

1*st*, To justify God in the dispensation, Psal. xxii. 3, and to submit to sovereignty, Job ii. 9, 10, believing he doth all things well. The man has to do with him whose will is the supreme law, and so must not adventure to call him to an account.

2*dly*, To cleave to God in Christ by a faith of adherence; saying with Job, "Though he slay me, yet will I trust in him, Job xiii. 15. He must resolutely adhere, over the belly of discouragements.

3*dly*, To believe an outgate in due time; saying with the church, Mic. vii. 8, "When I fall, I shall arise; when I sit in darkness, the Lord shall be a light unto me." Hence is that exhortation, Is. l. 10, "Who is among you that feareth the Lord, that obeyeth the voice of his servant, that walketh in darkness, and hath no light ? let him trust in the name of the Lord, and stay upon his God."

4*thly*, To hold the conclusion of our interest, notwithstanding the arguments drawn from the divine dispensation to prove us naught. Hence says Job chap. xxvii. 5, 6, "Till I die, I will not remove my integrity from me. My righteousness I hold fast, and will not let it go : my heart shall not reproach me so long as I live."

5*thly*, Continuing in the way of duty notwithstanding; as Job did, chap. i. 20, 21, who, notwithstanding all the calamites that befel him, blessed God.

Thirdly, There is a fight of faith in temptations from Satan. He is the declared enemy of God and mankind. Natural men he tempts to sin, to get them kept the surer in his gripes; the godly, that he may mar their communion with God, their comfort and growth, and may make their lives bitter, if he cannot get them back entirely to his service; both that he may get God dishonoured by them. The temptations of Satan are too many to be reckoned up particularly; but I shall take notice of these eight things following, in which ye would set yourselves to fight the fight of faith.

1. Temptations to sin, after some seeming or real enjoyment of God in ordinances or providences. Nothing is more ordinary than a subtile or furious attack of the devil on a person brought into a better case than ordinary, Cant. v. 1, 2. Thus after solemn ordinances. So after Christ's baptism, Matth. iv. 1; and the disciples after the first communion. Satan is a proud, envious Spirit. The better it is with a soul, the more likely is the honour of God to be advanced, and their own salvation. And neither of these can that malicious spirit endure. In this case faith is to manage a fight, by,

1st, Believing the Scripture warnings and instances of this: Luke xxii. 31, "And the Lord said, Simon, Simon, behold, Satan hath desired to have you, that he may sift you as wheat." 2 Cor. xii. 7. "And lest I should be exalted above measure through the abundance of the revelations, there was given to me a thorn in the flesh, the messenger of Satan to buffet me, lest I should be exalted above measure." Hereby the soul will be set to watch before the temptation come, and so be in better case to resist it; and when it is come, will see that it is no more than what God's people have met with.

2dly, Resisting, not in confidence of vows, purposes, and resolutions, the present frame of the heart, or grace already received; but in confidence of the grace that is in Christ, and the new supplies of it: 2 Cor. xii. 9, "My grace is sufficient for thee: for my strength is made perfect in weakness." 2 Tim. ii. 1, "Thou therefore, my son, be strong in the grace that is in Christ Jesus." It is confidence in what we have in ourselves that mars all.

2. Temptations to the sin that one is most easily laid aside unto: Heb. xii. 1, "Let us lay aside every weight, and the sin which doth so easily beset us." Satan will be sure to attack you on the weak side, where he is most likely to prevail. He knows what is the sin of one's constitution, age, calling, and the like, and there to set on where the wall is weakest. But he that minds for heaven, must resist, and fight against him, and that in faith.

1st, Believing the necessity of overcoming, even in that particular: Matth. v. 29, 30, "If thy right eye offend thee, pluck it out, and cast it from thee: for it is profitable for thee that one of thy members should perish, and not that thy whole body should be cast into hell. And if thy right hand offend thee, cut it off, and cast it from thee: for it is profitable for thee that one of thy members should perish, and not that thy whole body should be cast into hell." Men would do well to remember that there the one thing lacking, which ruins all, may lie, Mark x. 21. And if the devil can get the man kept under the dominion of any one lust, it will serve his purpose for that man's eternal ruin, though he have otherwise many good things about him.

2*dly*, Believing, that such temptations may be overcome and got mastered: Luke xvii. 6, "If ye had faith as a grain of mustard-seed, ye might say unto this sycamine-tree, Be thou plucked up by the root, and be thou planted in the sea; and it should obey you." These temptations men do so naturally incline to comply with, that they are ready to think, it is in vain to offer to resist them, for it will not do, Jer. ii. 25, "Thou saidst, There is no hope. No, for I have loved strangers, and after them will I go." This is the language of unbelief, which faith must contradict, if one would stand.

3*dly*, Believing, that, in the use of appointed means, he shall overcome, through grace and strength from the Lord: Mark xi. 24, "What things soever ye desire when ye pray, believe that ye receive them, and ye shall have them." This faith makes the soul in this case like a giant refreshed with wine, opposing Christ's promised strength to its own weakness, and the force of the temptation; and so brings it off victorious, Is. xl. ult. and xlv. 24.

3. Temptations to the grossest sins. Nobody is out of hazard of these, while in this world, 1 Cor. x. 12, "Let him that thinketh he standeth, take heed lest he fall." Satan makes great hellish gain by these; he wastes and defiles the conscience, gets God greatly dishonoured, and religion exposed to reproach by them. He gets the mask pulled off many hypocrites by them; and gets sincere Christians sometimes made to go halting to the grave by them, Prov. vii. 26. They that would see heaven must resist, and resist in faith,

1*st*, Believing that they are snares for soul-ruin, according to the word, Prov. vi. 27, 28, "Can a man take fire in his bosom, and his clothes not be burnt? Can one go upon hot coals, and his feet not be burnt?" and chap. i. 17, "Surely in vain the net is spread in the sight of any bird." It is the work of faith to discern, by the glass of the word, Satan's devices, and arts of destruction; that the soul, seeing them so, may conceive a horror of them. Hence says the apostle, Rom. xii. 9, "Abhor that which is evil."

2*dly*, Believing that it is not the temptation, but the yielding to it, that will provoke God against you. I own, that such temptations are often sent as a punishment for other sins, as Judas' covetousness was punished with a temptation to betray Christ for money: and by such means God often shakes himself loose of hypocrites, as in Judas' case, and spues them out of his mouth, leaving them to yield to them, Rev. iii. 16. And it is often the thought of serious souls, that temptations to sins so very gross are a sign of the Lord's hatred against them: yet that is a plain mistake; for what sin is there so gross but a child of God may be tempted to it? Asaph was tempted to deny a providence, Psal. lxxiii. 13. Agur saw himself in hazard of atheistical contempt of God, Prov. xxx. 9. Job was tempted to blaspheme and curse God, Job i. 11, 12. to self-murder, chap. vii. 15. Christ himself was tempted to distrust, self-murder, and worshipping of the devil, Matth. iv. The faith of these things will be strengthening under such horrid temptations.

3*dly,* Believing the word condemning and forbidding these sins, and so opposing Heaven's word of command and threatening unto the temptation. Thus our Lord resisted all his temptations in faith, Matth. iv. This is faith's wielding the sword of the Spirit against the tempter, which is fitted to awe the heart with the authority of God, and fill it with abhorrence of the temptation. Whenever the temptation is given, there should presently be some apt Scripture to oppose to it in faith; and as oft as the temptation is repeated, do ye repeat the word in faith, and Satan will fly at length. So in such cases ye should have such Scriptures as these ready, Deut. xxviii. 58, 59; Psal. xiv. 1; 1 John iii. 15; Eph. v. 5, 6.

4*thly,* Believing the promises suited to the case. There is no temptation any can be in, but there is a promise suited for it in the word, which is the armour faith must wield in order to overcome: 1 Cor. x. 13, God is faithful, who will not suffer you to be tempted above that ye are able; but will with the temptation also make a way to escape, that ye may be able to bear it." James iv. 7, "Resist the devil, and he will flee from you." And in the faith of the promise make resistance, not doubting but it shall be accomplished in your case: and according to your faith of the promise in the use of means, so shall it be; as with Peter on the water, and the army against Amalek with Moses' hands lift up.

4. Temptations artfully suited to one's circumstances. Satan has a hellish art of framing his temptations upon his observation of people's circumstances, wherein they are most likely to take with them. Thus Christ being an hungered, the devil tempted him to distrust, Matth. iv. 3. Job was tempted to blaspheme and despair under his afflictions. Achan was tempted to steal, a fair op-

portunity offering. Thus he has his temptations suited to the aged and the young, the poor and the rich, the jovial and those of a sorrowful heart. He knows, that in such a case he rows with the stream, and is most likely to prevail. But resist ye in faith,

1*st*, Believing, according to the word, that Satan watcheth all opportunities against you, 1 Pet. v. 8. "Be sober, be vigilant; because your adversary the devil, as a roaring lion, walketh about seeking whom he may devour." This will make you to watch against him, when the enemy has such an advantage against you that he will not let slip. They had not need to sleep who are within the enemy's gunshot.

2*dly*, Believing that God's eye is on you, and the Lord has you upon your trials in that particular, to which ye are so tempted. Hence says Joseph, Gen. xxxix. 9, "How can I do this great wickedness, and sin against God? Men's corrupt hearts are apt to think, when a fair occasion of sinning lies before them, that now is the time to gratify the lust; but happy were they could they think, now, here is a trial for me, and God is looking on to see how I will behave.

3*dly*, Believing that as the devil suits his temptations, so Christ suits his help and assistance, to the circumstances of poor sinners: so that resolving to resist, you may say, There are more with us than against us, 1 Cor. x. 13, forecited. Whatever way the stream runs for your compliance with the temptation, stretch out your withered hands to swim against it, in faith of your throughbearing upon the ground of God's faithfulness, Is. xl. 28—30.

5. Temptations from one sin to another. Satan knows, that one sin makes way for another; and that to get in his finger once, is the way to get in his whole hand after. So Eve's lustful look to the forbidden fruit, made way for her taking, taking for eating, that for giving to her husband and his eating: and so the whole world's ruin was completed, Gen. iii. 6. Thus it is usual for Satan to prevail with those that have yielded to him in one temptation, to lie for covering it again. And some sins natively lead to others; as in the well known story of the three sins one was tempted to. Thus drunkenness makes men an easy prey to uncleanness, Prov. xxiii. 33. And some when once the devil has got them to be harlots, the temptation from that, and from their credit, has made them murderers: some murdering their children after they are born, some before they are born, going about to destroy their conceptions; the latter as well as the former murderers, and guilty of innocent blood in a degree beyond Onan, Gen. xxxviii. 9, whom the Lord himself slew as a murderer. But ye must resist, and that in faith.

Happy they who resist the beginnings of sin, who crush the viper in the bud: but when ye are fallen into the snare, fight against the temptation to add sin to sin, or to cover one sin with another.

1*st*, Believing, that there is mercy for penitents, but none for those who harden themselves in their wickedness: Prov. xxviii. 13, "He that covereth his sins, shall not prosper: but whoso confesseth and forsaketh them, shall have mercy." Nay, there is not a more ready way under heaven to expose sinners to the arrows of God's wrath, than to be hardened in wickedness, Deut xxix. 19, 20.

2*dly*, Believing, that the design of the temptation to one sin from another, is plainly the ruin of the soul, that the devil may get the person so deep into the mire, that he may never win out again. Thus he drove Judas from the betraying of Christ, into an attack against his own life. For thus the one sin becomes a need-nail to the other, shutting up the soul under the guilt of it, not to be removed but by a miracle of mercy.

3*dly*, Believing, that all the shame, and pain, and misery that can follow in the world, upon one sin, is not to be laid in the balance with the wrath of God, that is kindled against the sinner by running into another sin because he has been guilty of one, Matth. xvi. 26. This all such as so do will find, either in this world, or in hell, when God shall make all their sins together lie on their own heads. For sooner or later sin will find out the guilty, Numb. xxxii. 23.

4*thly*, Believing the promise of pardon through the Redeemer's blood, however atrocious and heinous the sin is: 1 John i. 7, "The blood of Jesus Christ his Son cleanseth us from all sin." Some are led on from one sin to another, because they have no sense of the ill and danger of it to their souls: the faith of God's testimony of their sin would cure this, and make them cry out, Undone. Others have a secret despair of finding mercy, and so they proceed from evil to worse: but the faith of the promise of pardon would cure that: Is. i. 18, "Come now and let us reason together, saith the Lord: though your sins be as scarlet, they shall be as white as snow; though they be red like crimson, they shall be as wool."

5*thly*, Believing the promise of renewed strength even to those that have slighted it before, Jer. iii. 14. They who have been foiled by one temptation, may get victory over another. They may have taken a large step on the devil's ground, who yet looking to Christ by faith, may stop and go no further, Psal. lxv. 3.

6. Temptations suddenly and surprisingly cast in, and resolutely continued, 2 Cor. xii. 8. These are Satan's fiery darts, Eph. vi. 16. This is a furious assault of the devil, which he often makes use of in blasphemous or other diabolical injections into the minds of

poor sinners; where the soul is in no better case than one, who descending a thatched house, no sooner gets one fire-ball quenched, but another is thrown in on him. If at any time this be your case, set to vigorous resistance, in faith,

1*st*, Believing, that these are your affliction and trial, but no further your sin than you yield or consent to them. This is clear from the horrible Satanical suggestions made to our Saviour, Matt. iv. while yet there was no sin in him. Satan does with these as harlots laying their brats at the door of honest matrons, so confounding, perplexing, and hurrying the poor tempted sinner, that he is apt to take the voice of Satan for his own voice. But unless ye yield to them, and embrace them, Satan, and only he, shall be accountable for them.

2*dly*, Adhering resolutely by faith to the Lord Jesus, in that hour and power of darkness, as your Lord and Saviour did. Thus our Lord gave us an example, John xii. 27, "Now is my soul troubled; and what shall I say? Father, save me from this hour: but for this cause came I unto this hour." If ever that resolute adherence is necessary, it is necessary at such a time: Is. l. 10, "Who is among you that feareth the Lord, that obeyeth the voice of his servant, that walketh in darkness, and hath no light? let him trust in the name of the Lord, and stay upon his God." The great end and design of the tempter by these furious attacks, is, to drive the poor tossed tempted creature from his hold of Christ: but we should be like the traveller in the windy day, that holds his cloak the faster the harder it blows.

3*dly*, Believing, that there is no safety in parleying with the tempter, but ever and anon the temptation is to be rejected with abhorrence. It was Eve's parley with the tempter, that laid the foundation of the ruin of the world by the first sin, Gen. iii. Setting on the Second Adam, he got his answer a refusal, with abhorrence of his proposal, immediately, Matth. iv. These suggestions are not so far to be listened to, as that one should think with himself whether he should comply with them or not. "The Lord rebuke thee," is the short and safe answer.

4*thly*, Believingly opposing the Lord's word to them, which condemns and forbids the things tempted to. In those temptations our Saviour met with, which were shocking even to the light of nature, it is remarkable he still opposes scripture to them, Matth. iv. 7, 10. For that is a divine ordinance for repelling of temptation, to be reiterated in faith as often as Satan repeats his temptation.

5*thly*, Believing, that there is grace in Christ Jesus sufficient for repelling these most violent temptations, and that it is sufficient for you in your case in particular. Hence says our Lord, 2 Cor. xii. 9, "My grace is sufficient for thee: for my strength is made perfect in weakness." If Satan prevail so far as to cause the tempted to think, that the violence of the temptation is so great that it is not possible for them to stand against it; this is such a weakening of faith, that the breach can hardly miss to be made there, as a breaking forth of an high wall in an instant. And Satan cannot obtain it of the tempted but by turning his eyes away from Christ into himself. Therefore, in that hour of darkness, let the tempted keep his eye on the fulness of strength in Christ for him: 2. Tim. ii. 1, "Thou therefore, my son, be strong in the grace that is in Christ Jesus."

6*thly*, Believing the promise of victory to the poor struggler with temptation: Jam. iv. 7, "Resist the devil, and he will flee from you." The faith of the victory is necessary to animate the tempted to continue the struggle, and will make him in the temptation to be like a giant refreshed with wine, and will undoubtedly bring him off victorious at length. For there is the decision, "According to thy faith, so be it unto thee."

7. Temptations striking at the very foundations of faith and religion, such as against the being of God, and the divine authority of the scriptures, Psal. xiv. 1. and lxxiii. 13. These are most dangerous, but they are what the devil himself cannot prevail with himself to believe; though he fain would, yet he cannot be an atheist, nor an infidel as to the scriptures, Jam. ii. 19. But he sometimes would palm these foul atheistical principles on poor sinners, even saints of God, who want not an atheistical principle in them to work upon. If at any time Satan attack you with such temptations, ye must resist them,

1*st*, Believing, that they are the spawn of the old serpent in the corrupt heart, the hissing of the crooked serpent: Psal. xiv. 1, "The fool hath said in his heart, There is no God." Hence it is said of the beast in Rev. xiii. 6. that "he opened his mouth in blasphemy against God, to blaspheme his name, and his tabernacle, and them that dwell in heaven." This is the reception they should get immediately, faith discerning the devil's cloven foot in them at their very first appearance. Whether they come immediately from the devil, or from the corrupt heart itself moved by Satan, it is all a case in this point; believe them to be hellish, devilish, most abominable, and to be treated with the utmost abhorrence. And the sooner ye give them that entertainment, the victory will be the more easy and speedy.

2*dly*, Resolutely believing the foundation-principles which the temptation strikes against, over the belly of the Satanical objections mustered up against them before you, though ye be not able to answer those objections or loose the difficulties: Heb. xi. 6, "He that cometh to God, must believe that he is, and that he is a rewarder of them that diligently seek him." 2 Tim. iii. 16, "All scripture is given by inspiration of God, and is profitable for doctrine, for reproof, for correction, for instruction in righteousness." And hence is that exhortation of the apostle, Eph. vi. 16, "Above all, taking the shield of faith, wherewith ye shall be able to quench all the fiery darts of the wicked."

There is not wanting store of reasons to support the great foundation-principles of religion; and nothing but sophistry can be brought against them, which reason sufficiently enlightened may discover. There are convincing arguments for the being of a God, and the authority of the scriptures, to be used against atheists. But when ye are assaulted with these temptations, I dare not advise you to the way of disputing with the tempter, but to the way of believing; not to the bringing reasons for these principles against him, and answering his hellish objections against them, but to a resolute holding of the conclusion over the belly of all his objections; because,

(1.) They are first principles, and ye are not obliged to dispute them with any, unless it were to keep an opposer from ruin, as in the case of atheists. But this has no place in a combat with the devil, of whom there is no hope.

(2.) Because the devil is an intercommuned spirit, with whom we are not to commune and enter into reasoning without a special call. Our Lord himself, though he could have reasoned the devil out of it, yet he took not that method, but just opposed to his temptations the testimony of scripture. And it is certainly the safest way for us, whatever we have to say in temptation, to say it to God, rather than to the devil.

(3.) Because the devil is a disputant too subtle for us, and in the way of wit and reason may quickly over-reach us. I make no question, but the devil is a philosopher and divine far beyond any of our greatest scholars: and men may expect from him most subtle turns of wit to elude their arguments, and to start objections which it will not be easy to answer. And therefore it is not safe to engage in dispute with him.

But do ye resolutely believe the principles you have received on divine authority, which ye have no reason to quit on the devil's contrary testimony, though he pretend reason for it, since he is known to be a liar and murderer. This the apostle prescribes, Eph. vi. 16. forecited. And this method of holding by the conclusion resolutely, while the sinner is not capable to answer the objections, is recommended to us by the practice of the saints, Jer. xii. 1; Matt. xv. 25. Therefore, while Satan casts in these temptations, or raises them in your heart, enter your protestation against them, (crying out of violence and wrong), that you allow them not, you do believe, and will through his grace believe these foundations, and will not quit them.

3dly, Believing and applying the promise of saving illumination, and teaching of the Spirit. It is light from the Lord himself, that must dispel the mists that Satan raises in the corrupt heart, wherein these horrible temptations do take place. Hence says our Lord to Peter, Matth. xvi. 17, "Blessed art thou Simon Bar-jona: for flesh and blood hath not revealed it unto thee, but my Father which is in heaven." 1 Cor. ii. 12, "Now we have received, not the spirit of the world, but the spirit which is of God; that we might know the things that are freely given to us of God." And this light is brought in, by faith's applying the promises suited to the case. Of these are many, such as Heb. viii. 11; John 17, and xiv. 21. And the tempted should lift his eyes unto the Lord, that he may so shine in his word, into his soul, as that his light may dispel the darkness, according to his promise.

4thly, Believing the scripture accounts of these things, of those mysteries of providence from whence Satan raiseth these temptations. Satan sometimes observes the spirits even of saints fretted and rankled with long and sore afflictions, their prayers not heard and answered, the wicked prospering, and they in great distress; and here he plants his cannon, to beat down from these, even the foundations of all religion. Thus he dealt with Asaph, Psal. lxxiii. 12, 13, 14. And he resists him by believing the scripture account of those mysteries of providence, vers. 16—18. This is the way to undermine Satan's battery, to rase the foundations on which he builds.

What will that malicious spirit make of the long and sore distresses of God's people, and the prosperity of the wicked, against the being or nature of God, and the certainty of his word? The sun may hide his head long in a stormy winter; but will any say therefore, there is no sun, or that the ordinances of the heavens fail and misgive? Is not one day with the Lord as a thousand years, and a thousand years as one day? Doth not the scripture shew, that the wicked are raised on high, that they may fall more grievously? Is there not a judgment to come, and a long eternity enough to shew God's good pleasure in the vessels of his mercy, and his wrath against the vessels of wrath, though neither the godly have two summers, nor the wicked two winters, in one year? Have not prayers lain long over, that yet have got a gracious answer at length? Zech. vii. 3; James v. 11.

Thus believing is the method of resisting in these temptations. Howbeit, when ye are out of the shock of temptation in these matters, it would be of good use to fortify and confirm your faith of the foundation principles of religion, with all the reasons and arguments ye can draw together for them.

8. *Lastly*, Temptations of delusion. This is a kind of temptation most hard to resist, Satan therein transforming himself into an angel of light, and pressing to sin under the notion of duty, 2 Cor. xi. 14. It is a great trial of faith, Matth. xxiv. 24; a great and fearful plague where it takes, Is. lxvi. 4; 2 Thess. ii. 11, 12, and has always a lamentable upshot, according to the nature thereof, Is. l. ult. But ye must resist in faith,

1*st*, believing your own weakness and darkness in yourselves, together with the diligence of Satan the great seducer, according to the scripture, 2 Cor. iii. 5, "We are not sufficient of ourselves to think any thing as of ourselves: but our sufficiency is of God. 1 Pet. v. 8, "Be sober, be viligant; because your adversary the devil, as a roaring lion, walking about seeking whom he may devour." It is self-conceit, a high opinion of our own great attainments, that most readily betrays men into the snare of delusion; for these are in little fear of Satan's wiles, and so are the more easily caught in his snare.

2*dly*, Believing the holy scriptures to be the only rule of faith and manners, and a full and perfect rule; and to improve it so: Is. viii. 20, "To the law and to the testimony: if they speak not according to this word, it is because there is no light in them." There is an itch in the nature of man, to be wise above what is written; and sometimes Satan has made his gain thereof by visions, voices, dreams, impressions, and impulses. But in all such cases take head to yourselves, that Satan delude you not: but bring the matter to the word written, and thereby examine it. What is of God will abide the trial by that touch-stone; and the more closely it is brought to the word, it will appear the more clear: what is not so, will lose its lustre there, as ill wares brought out to the light of the sun. And therefore those under delusion are mighty loathe to examine by the word: 1 John iv. 1, "Beloved, believe not every spirit, but try the Spirits whether they are of God; because many false prophets are gone out into the world. 2 Pet. i. 18, 19, "And this voice which came from heaven we heard, when we were with him in the holy mount. We have also a more sure word of prophecy; whereunto ye do well that ye take heed, as unto a light that shineth in a dark place, until the day dawn, and the day-star arise in your hearts." The holy scripture is the stated way of communication betwixt heaven and us: it is from the Holy Spirit, and it is not possible that he should contradict himself, Is. lix. ult. Therefore "though we, or an angel from heaven, preach any other gospel unto you, than that which we have preached unto you, let him be accursed," Gal. i. 8.

Lastly, Believing the promise of guidance into all truth, John xvi. 13, "Howbeit, when he the Spirit of truth is come, he will guide you into all truth: for he shall not speak of himself; but whatsoever he shall hear, that shall he speak: and he will shew you things to come." Psal. xxv. 2, "The meek will he guide in judgment: and the meek will he teach his way." The soul thus emptied of itself, and leaning to the Lord Christ for his teaching, will not want teaching in the use of means. Hence says the Psalmist, Psal. xxviii. 7, "The Lord is my strength and my shield; my heart trusted in him, and I am helped." Our Lord Jesus is the appointed leader and guide of his people, Is. lv. 4. He is given of God for a light of the people. He has set us our ways-marks in this as in all other cases. Divine manifestations are always sanctifying and humbling; delusions puff up, and leave the soul always as unholy as they found it. Divine manifestations have ever an immediate tendency to holiness; delusions have always a tendency to unholiness. And even when duty is pressed in delusion, it will readily be found either out of season, or not the duty of one's station, or to have some such flaw in it or other.

Fourthly, There is a fight of faith in afflictions: Heb. x. 32, "Call to remembrance the former days, in which, after ye were illuminated, ye endured a great fight of afflictions." One may as well think to travel without the flies annoying him in a hot summer day, as to go through the world without meeting with afflictions. They are common to good and bad. In the Lord's way one cannot miss them: Acts xiv. 22, "We must through much tribulation enter into the kingdom of God." In the way of sin one will meet them too: Eccl. x. 8, "He that diggeth a pit, shall fall into it; and whoso breaketh an hedge, a serpent shall bite him." Sovereignty distributes them, to some more, to others less; but to all, some. The native effect of afflictions on the guilty creature, is to drive it away from God, (however they are oft turned to good); even as the lash of a whip natively drives away him that is lashed, from him that lasheth. So that it is owing to something else that they do good to sinners. And that,

1. To a word of divine appointment. Afflictions are an ordi-

nance of God for good to poor sinners: Is. xxvii. 9, "By this therefore shall the iniquity of Jacob be purged, and this is all the fruit to take away his sin." And a divine appointment will alter the nature and operation of a thing. The savour of burnt flesh is very unpleasant, but the divine ordinance of sacrificing made it a sweet savour, Gen. viii. 21. Clay laid on one's eyes is a mean natively to make one blind: yet, by virtue of a divine ordinance, it cured blindness, John ix. 6, 7. So afflictions natively, or of themselves, drive away the soul from God, but, by virtue of a divine ordinance, lead it to him.

2. To a receiving of them in faith: 2 Cor. iv. 17, 18, "For our light affliction, which is but for a moment, worketh for us a far more exceeding and eternal weight of glory; while we look not at the things which are seen, but at the things which are not seen: for the things which are seen, are temporal; but the things which are not seen, are eternal." See Heb. xi. 35—39. Whoever would profit by a divine ordinance, must receive it in faith, Heb. iv. 2. For to every divine ordinance there is a promise annexed to be believed: and the promise being believed, the ordinance has its effect. So that we see afflictions do good to some, to others no good, but ill: Why? It is faith and unbelief that make the difference.

Wherefore ye must fight in faith against the native tendency of afflictions in themselves. And if ye ask, What is that tendency in afflictions on the guilty creature, which he must fight against? and, How must one fight in faith against it? I answer in the six following particulars. It is,

1. To impress the person with the apprehension that God is his enemy, and that he is seeking his ruin: 2 Kings vi. ult. Even Job himself was carried away with this hard thought of God, Job xxxiii. 10, 11, "Behold, he findeth occasions against me, he counteth me for his enemy. He putteth my feet in the stocks, he marketh all my paths." Guilt lying on the conscience, makes it full of hard thoughts of God, and terrible forebodings. Whenever the guilty soul hears from heaven by affliction, it is ready to strike in his mind, Now this is for my sin, and God is proclaiming war against me to ruin me. Hence affliction is several times the means of awakening the secure sinner; though he can never come to God till he believe.

Now, ye must fight against this in faith,

1*st*, Believing, that though all your afflictions are infallible signs of God's hatred of your sin, and his seeking the ruin of it; yet no affliction on you in this world can be such a sign of God's hatred of your persons, and his seeking your ruin, Eccl. ix. 1, 2. No, no; God's dearest children may have as heavy afflictions on their backs, as any other persons in the world, Psal. lxxiii. 12, 14. And no wonder, since God's only begotten Son had the heaviest burden of afflictions that ever was on the back of a man.

2*dly*, Believing, that afflictions are God's ordinance for good to the afflicted, even as really as is the preaching of the word to them: Prov. xxix. 15, "The rod and reproof give wisdom." They are the discipline of God's house, as the word is the doctrine of it: Heb. xii. 6, "For whom the Lord loveth, he chasteneth, and scourgeth every son whom he receiveth." So the design of the rod is your good, as the design of physic is the health of the patient; though, in the meantime, one, by misguiding under it, may indeed kill himself; even as one, by not complying with the design of the affliction may wound his own soul. It is certain, that afflictions have a word of divine appointment for good; there is a blessing annexed to them by promise: but how can ye share of it, if ye do not believe them to be an ordinance of God for good?

3*dly*, Believing, that God by these means is seeking your good, as using towards you the very same means that he does towards the dearest of his children: 2 Pet. iii. 9, "The Lord is not slack concerning his promise, (as some men count slackness,) but is long-suffering to us-ward, not willing that any should perish, but that all should come to repentance." Rev. iii. 19, "As many as I love, I rebuke and chasten: be zealous therefore and repent." Should a physician give you the very same remedy that he gives to his own child, sick of your disease; what but unreasonable jealousy should make you think he designs ill to you? And what but unbelief then can it be that makes you think, that God seeks your ruin by affliction, with which he works the cure of his own?

4*thly*, Believing the promise annexed to that ordinance, with application to yourselves, that your affliction, through his grace, shall do you good: Is. xxvii. 9, "By this therefore shall the iniquity of Jacob be purged, and this is all the fruit to take away his sin." Zeph. iii. 12, 13, "I will also leave in the midst of thee an afflicted and poor people, and they shall trust in the name of the Lord. The remnant of Israel shall not do iniquity, nor speak lies: neither shall a deceitful tongue be found in their mouth: for they shall feed and lie down, and none shall make them afraid." This is the way to partake of the efficacy of the ordinance of affliction; and it is the faith of it that makes the saints welcome the rod, to be patient under it, and to comply with the design of it, Micah vii. 8, 9; while those that expect no good of them, get as little many times.

2. To take all heart and hand from him in his approaches to God. Hence says the Psalmist, Psal. lxxvii. 3, " I remembered God, and was troubled : I complained, and my spirit was overwhelmed. The guilty conscience takes up the affliction, and just knocks him down with it, fells him with it before the Lord. He is filled with consternation before an angry God, and his heart fails, and can look for no good at the Lord's hand, 1 John iii. 20, 21. The affliction lies so heavy upon the poor sinner, that he cannot think there is any hope of God's hearing his prayers, or making him welcome to the throne of grace. Hence says Job chap. ix. 16, 17, " If I had called, and he had answered me; yet would I not believe that he had hearkened unto my voice. For he breaketh me with a tempest, and multiplieth my wounds without cause." But ye must fight against this in faith,

1*st*, Believing, that there are bowels of compassion in God, while nothing but frowns appear (Psal. cxxx. 1, 7.) in his countenance. And it is faith's work, to take up these bowels of mercy in an afflicting God. QUESTION. What way shall one perceive them? ANSWER. While ye behold his anger in his providences, ye must look to his word by faith, and there ye will see these bowels of mercy: Is. xlix. 14—17, " But Zion said, The Lord hath forsaken me, and my Lord hath forgotten me. Can a woman forget her sucking child, that she should not have compassion on the son of her womb? yea, they may forget, yet will I not forget thee. Behold, I have graven thee upon the palms of my hands, thy walls are continually before me. Thy children shall make haste ; thy destroyers, and they that made thee waste, shall go forth of thee." Chap. lxiii. 9, " In all their affliction he was afflicted, and the angel of his presence saved them: in his love and in his pity he redeemed them, and he bare them, and carried them, all the days of old. And ye may be helped hereto, by considering the heart of a father smiting his own child ; where, in a sense, the heart goes not along with the hand. Thus the church prays, but in faith : Is. lxiii. 15, 16, " Look down from heaven, and behold from the habitation of thy holiness and of thy glory : where is thy zeal and thy strength, the sounding of thy bowels, and of thy mercies towards me ? are they restrained ? Doubtless thou art our father, though Abraham be ignorant of us, and Israel acknowledge us not : thou, O Lord, art our father, our redeemer, thy name is from everlasting." And this the church doth, and that on good grounds, Lam. iii. 33, " For he doth not afflict willingly [Heb. from his heart], nor grieve the children of men."

2*dly*, Believing the testimony of God's word, as to instances of persons that have had God's heart towards them, while his hand has been lying heavy on them. Thus it was with Gideon, Judg. vi. 12, 13. Thus it was with Job: he was most dear to God, yet he was given up unto the power of Satan to afflict him. And thus it was with a cloud of witnesses. These things are written for your learning; that ye, through patience and comfort of the Scriptures, might have hope.

3dly, Believing the promise of hearing the prayers of the afflicted, with application to yourselves: Psal. l. 15, "Call upon me in the day of trouble; I will deliver thee, and thou shalt glorify me." Oppose this promise in faith, to the disheartening operation of the affliction upon you before the Lord: take this cordial by the mouth of faith, when ye begin to faint in your approaches to God. So shall ye "lift up the hands that hang down, and the feeble knees." Is there a secret whisper, that you are so afflicted that you need not pray? It is the surmise of unbelief. Say ye, Since I am so afflicted, I am called to pray, James v. 13, "Is any among you afflicted? let him pray:" and there is a particular encouragement in my case, Psal. cii. 17, "He will regard the prayer of the destitute, and not despise their prayer."

3. To frighten the sinner away from God. Thus our first parents saw they were naked, and presently fled to hide themselves from the Lord. When the conscience is fired with guilt under affliction, its natural motion is to run away from God: 1 Sam. vi. 20, 21, "And the men of Bethshemesh said, Who is able to stand before this holy Lord God? and to whom shall he go up from us? And they sent messengers to the inhabitants of Kirjathjearim, saying, The Philistines have brought again the ark of the Lord; come ye down, and fetch it up to you." Hence the sorrow of the world is said to work death, because the more deep one is drenched in it, the farther he goes from God. Satan knows this very well, and therefore is he so eager to have sinners afflicted, and to make their lives bitter with it; though he is sometimes outshot in his own bow, as in Job's case. But ye must fight against this in faith,

1st, Believing, that God sends on afflictions, not to frighten the sinner from him, but to bring the sinner to him: Hos. iv. ult, "The wind hath bound her up in her wings, and they shall be ashamed because of their sacrifices," Chap. v. 1, "Hear ye this, O priests, and hearken, ye house of Israel, and give ye ear, O house of the king; for judgment is toward you, because ye have been a snare on Mizpah, and a net spread upon Tabor." It is indeed God's ordinary method to bring home runaways and backsliders: Hos. ii. 6, 7, "Therefore, behold, I will hedge up thy ways with thorns, and make a wall, that she shall not find her paths. And she shall follow after her lovers, but she shall not overtake them; and she shall seek them, but shall not find them: then shall she say, I will go and return to my first husband, for then was it better with me than now." Satan's design is one thing in them, and God's design another: and though Satan row with the stream, a touch from the hand of God on the sinner's heart will carry his purpose.

2*dly*, Believing, that none can better their case by running away from the Lord: however hard their case may seem with him, they can never mend themselves at another hand. Hence said Samuel unto the people, 1 Sam. xii. 21, "Turn ye not aside: for then should ye go after vain things, which cannot profit nor deliver, for they are vain." And hence we find, that Peter said to Christ, John vi. 68, "Lord to whom shall we go? thou hast the words of eternal life." The sinner under affliction is often like Hagar, "flying from the face of her mistress Sarai, Gen. xvi. 8: and that is the best course which the angel of the Lord directed Hagar unto, ver. 9 namely, to return to her mistress, and submit herself under her hands. Jonah fled from the presence of the Lord, and shunning the journey to Nineveh, cast himself into a whale's belly. And those that take course in their affliction, will not speed better.

3*dly*, Believing your welcome unto, and certain reconciliation with an offended God through Christ, 2 Cor. v. 19, 20, "God was in Christ, reconciling the world unto himself, not imputing their trespasses unto them; and hath committed unto us the word of reconciliation. Now then we are ambassadors for Christ, as though God did beseech you by us: we pray you in Christ's stead, be ye reconciled to God." God was never so angry with any of Adam's children, but he was ready to lay by his anger for the sake of Christ, apprehended by faith. The whole tenor of the gospel holds out this truth: and the law is suffered to lash the sinner, and afflictions are laid on him, to the very end that he may improve it for his reconciliation with God.

4. To bring the sinner to cast off religion, and to lay aside the duties of it. Hence says Christ of the stony ground hearers, Matth. xiii. 21, "When tribulation or persecution ariseth because of the word, by and by they are offended." Thus we find a profane generation arguing the vanity of religion, and the duties of it, from their afflicted and low circumstances, Mal. iii. 14, 15, "Ye have said, It is vain to serve God: and what profit is it, that we have kept his ordinance, and that we have walked mournfully before the Lord of hosts? And now we call the proud happy: yea, they that work wickedness are set up; yea, they that tempt God are even de-

livered." No less a man than Asaph was near to have turned atheist on this very score, under a strong temptation, Psal. lxxiii. 12, 13, 14, "Behold," says he, "these are the ungodly, who, prosper in the world they increase in riches. Verily I have cleansed my heart in vain, and washed my hands in innocency. For all the day long have I been plagued, and chastened every morning." And so it has fared with many, who in their prosperity have kept up a form of religion, that their spirits have been quite soured as to religion in their adversity, and they have visibly given up with it; like the mixed multitude in the wilderness.

Here is great need to fight the fight of faith,

1*st*, Believing that prosperity is not tied to religion, nor yet to irreligion: but which of the ways soever one takes, affliction will meet him in the world, Eccl. ix. 2, "All things come alike to all; there is one event to the righteous and to the wicked," &c. If men take up religion for worldly prosperity, no wonder they be baulked of their expectation, and lay it aside again upon the disappointment. But their laying it aside will not secure them from affliction. Therefore men should look so to religion itself, as to be wedded to it for its instrinict value. But in the way of religion men may find a good conscience under affliction, while they find an ill conscience in the way of casting it off.

2*dly*, Believing that the great advantage of religion is to be reaped after the time of trial in this life is over. Hence says our Lord, Rev. ii. 10, "Be thou faithful unto death, and I will give thee a crown of life." Chap. iii. 21, "To him that overcometh will I grant to sit with me in my throne, even as I also overcame, and am set down with my Father in his throne." Now is our seed-time; and the sowing must be in tears, where the reaping time of joy is to follow. The harvest of glory in heaven comes most full after a wet seed-time.

3*dly*, Believing that there is a notable advantage in religion for bearing of afflictions. Hence says the apostle, 2 Cor. i. 12, "Our rejoicing is this, the testimony of our conscience, that in simplicity and godly sincerity, not with fleshly wisdom, but by the grace of God, we have had our conversation in the world, and more abundantly to you-wards." There are promises in the covenant, which applied by faith, are full of comfort to the afflicted. The Lord's word is full of light as to the nature, uses, and ends of them; so that the Bible is the best company for those in affliction. This well is deep and faith must draw.

4*thly*, Believing that the promises with respect to affliction, both as to the blessed issue of them in another world, and as to support under them in this world, shall be made out to you. Thus Asaph in his affliction fastened his feet, Psal. lxxiii. 24, "Thou shalt guide me with thy counsel," says he, "and afterward receive me to glory." It is the faith of the upper Canaan, and of provision in the wilderness-world, that fits for the wilderness-life.

5. To provoke the sinner against God, to cause him to murmur against him, quarrel with him, and arraign and condemn in his heart, at least, the conduct of holy providence in the ordering of his lot: 1 Cor. x. 10, "Neither murmur ye, as some of them also murmured, and were destroyed of the destroyer." Prov. xix. 3, "The foolishness of man perverteth his way: and his heart fretteth against the Lord." Hard affliction laid on a man in whom dwelleth a corrupt heart, is apt to raise the black band of impatience, complaining, fretting, murmuring, and practical blashemy against God; like a stick stirring up a muddy pool, or an ant's nest. It made even a Job and Jeremiah to curse the day of their birth. Job was much overcome with his affliction, when he expressed himself so indecently, chap. xxx. 21, "Thou art become cruel to me: with thy strong hand thou opposest thyself against me." Fight against this tendency of affliction in faith,

1*st*, Believing, that God is a righteous God, and your Sovereign Lord, having all power over you. There may be mysteries of providence in his dealing with us, which we cannot account for: but there can be no unjust step in his procedure with us: Deut. xxxii. 4, "He is the rock, his work is perfect: for all his ways are judgment: a God of truth, and without iniquity, just and right is he." Therefore that conclusion must be stuck to by faith, Jer. xii. 1, "Righteous art thou, O Lord, when I plead with thee." We are his own by creation, and have forfeited our mercies by sin: let faith view him in the throne of sovereignty, and silence us: Matth. xx. 15, "Is it not lawful for me to do what I will with mine own?"

2*dly*, Believing, that you are debtors to mercy for that it is not worse with you than it is; saying, with the church, Lam. iii. 22, "It is of the Lord's mercies that we are not consumed, because his compassions fail not." However hard any one's affliction is in this world, it is certain they deserve worse, and God could lay on worse. Hence is that acknowledgment of Ezra's, chap. ix. 13, "Thou our God hast punished us less than our iniquities deserve;" and that, Psal. xc. 11, "Who knoweth the power of thine anger? even according to thy fear, so is thy wrath." This will make one to give thanks for what is kept off, rather than murmur for what is laid on.

3*dly*, Believing, that there is certainly need for all you meet with: 1 Pet. i. 6, "Wherein ye greatly rejoice, though now for a season [if need be] ye are in heaviness through manifold temptations." A holy wise God lays no needless afflictions on any: Lam. iii. 33, "For he doth not afflict willingly, nor grieve the children of men." Nay he gives all by weight and measure, and will not put in one grain beyond what the case requires. What though ye cannot see it? ye have yet ground to believe it from the word, and may see it in the glass of God's infinite wisdom, the contrivance of which your lot is, Deut. xxxii. 4. So that whatsoever he doth to you, is not only well done, but best done in your circumstances, Eccl. iii. 14.

4*thly*, Believing, that, through the grace of our Lord Jesus, all you meet with shall work for your good: Rom. viii. 28, "We know," says the apostle, "that all things work together for good, to them that love God, to them who are the called according to his purpose." God can carry on the good of a person, by that which he is apt to think is for his ruin; as was the case with Jacob, when he said unto his sons, Gen. xlii. 36, "Me have ye bereaved of my children: Joseph is not, and Simeon is not, and ye will take Benjamin away: all these things are against me." And though the good of them may be long ere it appear, yet where it is believed and hoped for, it will come at length, Jam. v. 7. Now this and all other promises is held forth to you in Christ to be believed, and applied to yourselves.

6. *Lastly*, To cause the sinner harden himself in sorrow. So we render that expression of Job's, chap. vi. 10, "I would harden myself in sorrow;" But it is not the sense of that place. Affliction had this bad effect on good Jacob, Gen. xxxvii. 35. who, when all his sons, and all his daughters, rose up to comfort him concerning the loss of his son Joseph, "refused to be comforted; and said, For I will go down into the grave unto my son, mourning." It had also this bad effect on Asaph, Psal. lxxvii. 2, "In the day of my trouble I sought the Lord," says he; "my sore ran in the night, and ceased not: my soul refused to be comforted." Under affliction the heart is apt to sink; and the case sometimes appears so hopeless, that the afflicted looks not after comfort, but staves it off when offered. They bid a solemn farewell as it were to joy and comfort, and draw the sable curtains of sorrow about themselves: they have no comfortable prospect, they look for none, and resolve to hold there. This is dangerous. Fight against it in faith,

1*st*, Believing the promise of a comfortable outgate at length, with application to your own case. This hardening one's self in sorrow, whatever be the probabilities it is founded on, is the proper fruit of unbelief, and casts discredit on the promises of God, Psal. ciii. 9, "He will not always chide; neither will he keep his anger for ever." Lam. iii. 32, "But though he cause grief, yet will he have compassion according to the multitude of his mercies." It is faith's work to believe the accomplishment of them, though one cannot see how.

2*dly*, Believing the promise of a comfortable mixture in the affliction while it lasts. God has given a promise of moderating the trials of believers: Psal. xxxvii. 24, "Though he fall, he shall not be utterly cast down; for the Lord upholdeth him with his hand." Is. xxxvii. 8, "In measure when it shooteth forth, thou wilt debate with it; he stayeth his rough wind in the day of the east wind." And they have had experience of the outmaking thereof, 2. Cor. iv. 8, 9, "We are troubled on every side, yet not distressed, (says the apostle); we are perplexed, but not in despair; persecuted, but not forsaken; cast down, but not destroyed." God has given a promise of strengthening believers to bear their trials, Deut. xxxiii. 27, "The eternal God is thy refuge, and underneath are the everlasting arms. Is. xl. 28, 29, 30, 31, "Hast thou not known? hast thou not heard, that the everlasting God, the Lord, the Creator of the ends of the earth, fainteth not neither is weary? there is no searching of his understanding. He giveth power to the faint; and to them that have no might, he increaseth strength. Even the youths shall faint and be weary, and the young men shall utterly fall. But they that wait upon the Lord, shall renew their strength: they shall mount up with wings as eagles, they shall run and not be weary, and they shall walk and not faint." The Psalmist experienced the accomplishment of this promise, Psal. cxxxviii. 3, "In the day when I cried, thou answeredst me, (says he): and strengthenedst me with strength in my soul." God has given a promise of cordials now and then to support them, sweet blinks now and then to refresh them: Hos. ii. 14, "Therefore, behold, I will allure her, and bring her into the wilderness, and speak comfortably unto her." Micah vii. 8, "Rejoice not against me, O mine enemy: when I fall, I shall arise, when I sit in darkness, the Lord shall be a light unto me."

3*dly*, Believing, that your patient suffering of affliction is as acceptable to God through Christ, as your doing for God: 2 Tim. ii. 12, "It is a faithful saying, If we suffer, we shall also reign with him." God has several pieces of work that he puts into the hands of his people: some he calls to do great things, others to suffer great things, Heb. xi. Whatever it is the Lord carves out to you, ply that; it is what God will accept at thy hand through the Mediator. Suffering is as really service to God, as doing is.

Thus we have seen the evil tendency of afflictions in themselves, and how we are to fight against it by faith. But there are three special cases wherein that force of affliction is greater than ordinary, and requires a strong faith to stand the shock.

1. When a stroke from the hand of the Lord comes upon a man in the way of his duty, which he is doing in obedience to the call and command of God. This is apt to make a stagger, especially when it is a duty others have an ill eye on: for by it God seems to give sentence against the man and his work. When people are going on in an ill way, it is no wonder Heaven works against them; but when the Lord meets a man as an enemy in the way of duty, that is a great trial, Psal. lxxi. 11. It is apt to make one leave duty.

Here is great need to fight in faith,

1*st*, Believing, that that is no sign that the way you are in, being warranted by the word, is displeasing to God. It has been the trial of the Lord's people, when they have been called to the plainest duty, and have been upon signal pieces of service to God. We are to observe providences, but not to make a Bible of them; but bring them to the word, and that will open the mysteries of providence. Jonah seemed to be favoured by providence when he set his face to go to Tarshish, Jon. i. 3, yet he was wrong. Jacob had God's call to return to his own country, and a promise of the Lord's being with him, Gen. xxxi. 3. Laban looked on it with an ill eye. But what a train of troubles met he with in his way thither? such as his meeting with Esau, his thigh put out of joint in wrestling with the angel, his domestic trials, &c. And you may read the trials Moses met with in his going down to Egypt, upon God's command to redeem the Israelites, Exod. iv. 24, &c.

2*dly*, Believing, that God has holy designs in the matter, becoming his own infinite wisdom, which ye may afterwards come to see, if ye see them not in the time; though in the meantime he is pleased with your way. Hence said our Lord to Peter, John xiii. 7, " What I do thou knowest not now; but thou shalt know hereafter." Sometimes he designs to correct for some mismanagement in the setting about the duty, as in Moses' case for not circumcising his son, Exod. iv. 24, 25; sometimes to hide pride from men's eyes, as in the apostle's case, 2 Cor. xii. 7, and as in the case of the children of Israel their being foiled by the children of Benjamin, Judg. xx. 18—26. And this he doth always for the trial of his people, their faith, regard to duty, &c. So Satan may be permitted to act against them for their trial; and sure he will be the more eager, the more important the duty is, 1 Cor. xvi. 9; 1 Thess. ii. 18.

3*dly*, Believing, that there is no safety in one's leaving the road of duty, meet with what they will in it. Hence says the wise man, Prov. x. 9, "He that walketh uprightly, walketh surely: but he that perverteth his ways shall be known." A rebuke in the way of duty is sweeter than a warm sunshine in the way of sin: "Moses esteemed the reproach of Christ greater riches than the treasures in Egypt, Heb. xi. 26. There is communion with God to be had in such providences, and they furnish men with useful experiences for their after life.

2. When the affliction is extraordinary, and unusual, so that it draws the eyes of beholders to notice it particularly. When people's afflictions are no more than what is very ordinary and usual, they are the more easily borne; but when God seems to point out one to others, by some unordinary stroke, how hard is that to bear, how hard to keep off concluding that God has a particular hatred against us? There is need to fight in faith here,

1*st*, Believing, that it has been often the lot of God's children, and particularly of his darling children whom he loved most to meet with such kind of trials as would seem to have imported a particular hatred of them. Hence says the apostle, Heb. x. 33, "Ye were made a gazing stock, both by reproaches and afflictions." And again, 1 Cor. iv. 9, "I think that God hath set forth us the apostles last, as it were appointed to death. For we are made a spectacle unto the world, and to angels, and to men." This was the lot of Christ himself, Psal. xxii. 6, "I am a worm, and no man," says he; "a reproach of men, and despised of the people." How was Job's heart pierced with that question, Job v. 1, "Call now, if there be any that will answer thee; and to which of the saints wilt thou turn? It is very rare, I suppose, that any of God's children have something more than ordinary about them to the advantage, but they get something more than ordinary to try them. Of all the patriarchs there was not one that had more divine manifestations or so many as Jacob, nor so many and great afflictions neither. Of all the sons of Jacob, there was none so high raised and useful as Joseph, and none so afflicted. Heman was a man of a more than ordinary reach, 1 Kings iv. 31, and so of afflictions, Psal. lxxxviii. 15, "I am afflicted" says he "and ready to die, from my youth up: while I suffer thy terrors, I am distracted." Moses was the meekest man in the earth, and never mere man had more ado with it; Job was the mirror of patience, and none suffered more.

2*dly*, Believing the illimited power of sovereignty, which requires absolute resignation: Matt. xx. 15, " Is it not lawful for me to do what I will with mine own?" It is a silencing query, Rom. ix. 20, "Nay but, O man, who art thou that repliest against God? shall the thing formed say to him that formed it, Why hast thou made me thus?" Sovereignty takes one piece of clay, and sets it on a throne; another of the same, and sets it on a dunghill in rags and sores; reaches to some the ordinary meal of affliction, but makes another's mess five times as much. And who will set bounds to the disposals of sovereignty?

3*dly*, Believing, that these different aspects of providence upon men, are but for a time, for the time of trial: and they will soon be at an end: Job xxi. 23—26, "One dieth in his full strength, being wholly at ease and quiet. His breasts are full of milk, and his bones are moistened with marrow. And another dieth in the bitterness of his soul, and never eateth with pleasure. They shall lie down alike in the dust, and the worms shall cover them." It is no great matter whether one be the king or the fool on the stage; for in a little they get behind the curtains, and each one appears as really he is. Ordinary and unordinary afflictions will shortly have an end; and they that bear their own part right, happy will they be.

3. When the affliction is of long continuance. Some afflictions are like a summer-shower, heavy in their time, but soon over, and it grows fair again: but the most trying are the continuing afflictions, that are like a stormy winter, that blows hard day after day. Many times deliverance is looked for, but it comes not. Any promising signs that appear at any time do misgive: and the storm is renewed, and grows ever the longer the more hopeless. Here is a sore shock to abide, which requires to fight in faith,

1*st*, Believing that this is a part of the discipline of God's house, whereby he exercises his own children. Hence says the prophet, Jer. viii. 20, "The harvest is past, the summer is ended, and we are not saved." David complains, Psal. lxix. 3. of his being weary of his crying, of his throat's being dried; of his eyes failing while he waited for his God. The church was so long continued in affliction, that she forgot prosperity, Lam. iii. 17. Many of the Lord's people have been kept so long under the hatches, that they have hung up their harps on the willows, so as to have no more use for them; and yet have been delivered.

2*dly*, Believing that the longest and blackest night will have a morning; and that though the affliction continue long, it will not continue always. Hence says the Psalmist, Psal. ciii. 9, "The Lord will not always chide: neither will he keep his anger for ever." If the question be, "Watchman, what of the night? watchman, what of the night?" Is. xxi. 11. the answer is, ver. 12, "The morning cometh, and also the night: if ye will inquire, inquire ye: return, come." The sky that has long lowred, may clear ere night: the wound may be looked on as incurable, that yet will be fairly healed, Jer. xv. 18, 20. And if it should not be removed in time, yet the faith of a blessed eternity may keep up the heart, when "God shall wipe away all tears from the eyes; and there shall be no more death, neither sorrow, nor crying, neither shall there be any more pain: for the former things are passed away," Rev. xxi. 4.

3dly, Believing that God knows the fittest season for removing the affliction, and not we. Hence said our Lord to his brethren, in another case, John vii. 6, "My time is not yet come: but your time is always ready." He keeps times and seasons in his own hand, and at the fit time he will remove it, Hab. ii. 3. but not before, if it is to be removed in mercy. Men's hearts must abide much hewing, and God may have much ado with an affliction that is not soon done. The affliction is too soon over, that is removed ere the design of it be answered, Psal. x. 17. None blames the husbandman, that he sows not his seed, before the ground be fit to receive it.

Lastly, Believing that the more we are resigned to the Lord as to the time and method of deliverance, the nearer we are to it, the fairer we lie for it. Hence says the Psalmist, Psal. x. 17, "Lord, thou hast heard the desire of the humble: thou wilt prepare their heart, thou wilt cause thine ear to hear." Man's extremity is God's opportunity, Deut. xxxii. 36. Witness Abraham on the mount, the disciples at sea, the Israelites at the Red sea. Happy should they be, who leaving the deliverance on the Lord, should make it their main care to answer the calls of providence by the affliction while it is continued.

Fifthly, There is a fight of faith with this present evil world." Hence says the apostle, 1 John v. 4, 5, "Whatsoever is born of God, overcometh the world: and this is the victory that overcometh the world, even our faith. Who is he that overcometh the world, but he that believeth that Jesus is the Son of God?" This present evil world is a party opposite to God and Christ, and on the devil's side: insomuch that he that lives in friendship with it, lives at enmity with God, James iv. 4. And therefore we must either fight against it, or be ruined by it. And there are these two particulars in the world, that we must fight the fight of faith against: 1. The things, 2. The men of the world.

1*st*, The things of the world are dangerous enemies to our souls, because of the corruption of our hearts. Hence says the apostle, 1 John ii. 15, "Love not the word, neither the things that are in the world. If any man love the world, the love of the Father is not in him." O the fearful havoc of souls that is made thereby! By them many saints have been cast down, wounded, and many sinners have been slain thereby. The things of the world set out three bands against us, whom we must either fight and overcome by faith, or be ruined by.

1. The white band of the world's smiles.
2. The black band of the world's frowns.
3. The mixed band of the world's cares.

First, The things of the world set out the white band of the world's smiles. And they are stained with the blood of many souls: Prov. i. 32, "For the turning away of the simple shall slay them, and the prosperity of fools shall destroy them." The smiling world does with other men, as the panther is said to do with other beasts. He draws them after him with the sweet smell of his breath, hiding his head, and afterwards devours them. Thus was Demas ruined. The white band fights against souls with two kinds of weapons.

1. Profits of the world. Thus it set upon poor Judas with thirty pieces of silver, and so knocked him down, and slew him. It set on Moses with the treasures of Egypt, and had done so to him, had he not had faith to resist it, Heb. xi. 26. The Psalmist observes the snare in these, and therefore gives the watchword, Psal. lxii. 10, "Trust not in oppression, and become not vain in robbery: if riches increase, set not your heart upon them." And many a man, who has stood his ground against the black band of the world's frowns, has been overcome with the white, like the man in the fable with the sun and the wind.

2. Pleasures of the world. There are three kinds of them; "the lust of the flesh, and the lust of the eyes, and the pride of life," 1 John ii. 16. These are the silken cords, with which souls are drawn to destruction: wherewith when once men come to be bound, they are like iron fetters; the breaking of which, if ever they be broken at all, will cost a flood of tears. Hence prays the penitent Psalmist, Psal. li. 8, "Make me to hear joy and gladness; that the bones which thou hast broken, may rejoice." With many they end in a judicial up-giving to vile affections, Rom. i. 26.

These weapons are wielded two ways.

(1.) In expectation. It is the natural desire of all men, "Who will shew us any good?" Psal. iv. 6. The world steps in and makes such an offer, as Satan did to Christ; who when he had "taken him into an exceeding high mountain, and shewed him all the kingdoms of the world, and the glory of them, said unto him, All these things will I give thee, if thou wilt fall down and worship me," Matth. iv. 8, 9. And when once the hope and expectation of its profits and pleasures is greedily embraced by an inordinate affection, the soul is set on fire therewith, and the poor creature runs to its own ruin on its own feet, Prov. vii. 22, 23. And so it fares with many in this case; as with the mouse, who, watching for the gaping oyster, thrusts in her head presently when the shell opens; which being immediately closed again, she is crushed. Hence says the apostle, 1 Tim. vi. 9, "They that will be rich, fall into temptation, and a snare, and into many foolish and hurtful lusts, which drown men in destruction and perdition."

(2.) In fruition or enjoyment, Luke xviii. 24, "And when Jesus saw that he was very sorrowful, he said, How hardly shall they that have riches enter into the kingdom of God?" Such is the corruption of the heart in man, that it is ten to one if the smiling world draw not his heart away from God. Men are apt to love the world inordinately, even when it gives them gall to drink: how hard must it be not to be overcome with it, when it courts men, and lays itself in their bosom! Deut. xxxiii. 15, "But Jeshurun waxed fat, and kicked: thou art waxed fat, thou art grown thick, thou art covered with fatness; then he forsook God which made him, and lightly esteemed the Rock of his salvation."

Ye must fight against the smiling world by faith if ever ye would have the smiles of the Lord's countenance,

1*st*, Believing the danger that is in the world's smiles, to your immortal souls. The danger is in the soul's being thereby drawn to sin against God, and so in end to be pierced with sorrows. Agur saw this, and believed it; and therefore prays thus, Prov. xxx. 8, 9, "Give me neither poverty, nor riches, feed me with food convenient for me; lest I be full, and deny thee, and say, Who is the Lord?"— The smiling world is apt to betray men into pride, and a high conceit of themselves, forgetting God, contempt of God's laws, giving up themselves to the swing of their corrupt lusts and affections, &c., and so to work the ruin of the soul, Eccl. v. 13. Believe this on the testimony of God and so shall ye we watch against it,

2*dly*, Believing the vanity, emptiness, and insufficiency, that is in the world, and all the smiles thereof: Psal. cxix. 96, "I have seen an end of all perfection, (says the Psalmist;) but thy commandment is exceeding broad." Eccl. i. 2, "Vanity of vanities, saith the preacher, vanity of vanities, all is vanity." What do they avail to a man's real worth? what can they contribute to one's eternal happiness? They are uncertain, and may quickly leave us, and will certainly leave us at length; we must go as we came, naked, Prov. xxiii. 5. They are insufficient, they cannot give ease to the heart of man; one dead fly may spoil all the pot of ointment, as in Haman and Ahab's case. They cannot satisfy the soul; witness the disappointment which the rich man met with, spoke of Luke xii. 16, &c.

3dly, Believing the trascendent profit and pleasure, that is to be had in the favour of God, the smiles of his countenance, communion and fellowship with him through Jesus Christ. This believe; and believe, that ye may have it, yea, that ye shall have it, seeking it through Christ: and ye shall overcome the smiling world. Hence says the Psalmist, Psal. iv. 6, 7, " Lord, lift thou up the light of thy countenance upon us. Thou hast put gladness in my heart, more than in the time that their corn and wine increased." Being thus by faith lifted up in your affections to heaven, the earth and all that is in it, will appear very little in your eyes, Matth. xiii. 45, 46; Philip. iii. 8. It is unbelief of, and blindness to the things of a better world, that makes the present evil world so bulky with men.

4thly, Believing the sufficiency of his grace to carry you above them: 2 Cor. xii. 9, "And he said unto me, My grace is sufficient for thee; for my strength is made perfect in weakness." There is strength in the Mediator, for men's overcoming the world: believe the promise with application to yourselves, and ye shall be more than conquerors. The promise brings salvation with it; and the faith of it loosed Zaccheus' heart from the world, Luke xix. 8.

Secondly, The things of the world set out the black band of the world's frowns. The world ofttimes brings up a train of crosses against men, to drive them away from God. Hence we read of the apostles " confirming the souls of the disciples, and exhorting them to continue in the faith, and that we must through much tribulation enter into the kingdom of God," Acts xiv. 22. Men must lay their accounts with their ilk days cross: and sometimes all goes wrong together with them; their sun goes down at noon-day, as in Job's case. Crosses in worldly things do often much mischief to the soul; they will irritate their corruptions, discompose them for duty to God, and lead them aside into manifold temptations, Prov. xxx. 9.

Some have a fighting life with the world all their days: but, alas! it is not the fight of faith with it, but a sinful faithless fighting with it, that carries on the ruin of their souls. Ye will know this faithless fight with it by these two things.

1. All their fight is to get something of the world, not to be kept from the spiritual evil of the world. The world does not prosper

with them, as it does with some others: and all their concern is to make a shift for throughbearing, which swallows up all other concerns with them. So they are such sons of earth, as that they live as if the curse of the serpent were lying on them, all their days to go on their belly, and lick the dust. The world flies from them; and yet they court it above all things. God crosses them in it, to bring their hearts off it; but over the belly of all the rebukes of providence, it is their great pursuit, Jer. v. 3, 4.

2. Their fight they have with the world, takes away from them all favour of the word of God, and of religion. A sad instance of this ye have, Exod. vi. 9, where, when Moses had spoken to the children of Israel all the promises commanded him of God, mentioned in the preceding verses, it is said, "But they hearkened not unto Moses, for anguish of spirit, and for cruel bondage." The fight of faith with the world makes the gospel savoury to men: but this carnal fight with it makes it sapless and tastelesss; it rankles their spirits with respect to religion, that many such are not far from thinking that religion is for the wealthier sort; but that as for them, they have another thing ado. And thus the frowning world ruins soul and body to them; at once ruins them for time and eternity.

I would advise you to another sort of fighting with the frowning world. Fight in faith against it,

1*st*, Believing that the ordering of your lot is in the hand of a holy wise God, who knows best what lot is for you, Job i. 21, whether prosperous or cross. The faith of this would make you embrace the world's frowns, and welcome crosses in the world, as well as prosperity, as what God sees meet for you; as did Job, chap. i. 21, who said, "Naked came I out of my mother's womb, and naked shall I return thither: the Lord gave, and the Lord hath taken away; blessed be the name of the Lord."

2*dly*, Believing that the world's frowns, and smiles too, are but empty and passing shews, which will be soon buried in everlasting forgetfulness. As the world's smiles appear more pleasant than indeed they are, so its frowns appear more terrible to the carnal heart, than they are really: Eccl. i. 2, "Vanity of vanities, saith the preacher, vanity of vanities, all is vanity." The one and the other are like foam on the water, appearing big, but soon pass away. Being seen by the eye of sense, O how weighty are they! But look to them with an eye of faith, and ye will see they are all but empty noise, which will quickly be laid, 2 Cor. iv. 17. The longest term of their continuance is but a few years at most. When one comes to the grave, the rich and poor are alike there; the black band and the white band are both disbanded there.

3*dly*, Believing that ye have greater things to be taken up about, than either the world's smiles or frowns. Hence says the Psalmist, Psal. iv. 6, 7, "Lord, lift thou up the light of thy countenance upon us. Thou hast put gladness in my heart, more than in the time that their corn and their wine increased." The one cannot make you happy, nor the other miserable. But the favour of God and his wrath are matters of weight; let it be your care to obtain the one, and escape the other. These things are eternal, the other but temporal; O slight not then the substance, with your concern for the shadow: Matt. xvi. 26, "For what is a man profited, if he shall gain the whole world, and lose his own soul? or what shall a man give in exchange for his soul?"

4*thly*, Believing that you are in yourselves unworthy of the least smile of common providence. Hence says Jacob, Gen. xxxii. 10, "I am not worthy of the least of all the mercies, and of all the truth, which thou hast shewed unto thy servant; for with my staff I passed over this Jordan, and now I am become two bands." And says the church, Lam. iii. 22, "It is of the Lord's mercies that we are not consumed, because his compassions fail not." O why do crosses in the world go so deep with men, but because of the want of due humiliation? and whence is that want, but from unbelief? The humble soul fighting with the world will surely be victorious, because however it frowns on him, he takes it kindly out of the hand of the Lord, as not worthy of better.

5*thly*, Believing that your souls are in hazard by the frowning world, as well as the souls of others by the fawning world. Hence is that prayer of Agur's, Prov. xxx. 8, 9, "Give me neither poverty, nor riches, feed me with food convenient for me.—lest I be poor, and steal, and take the name of my God in vain." The devil holds some fast in the iron chains of worldly adversity, as well as he does others in the golden chains of prosperity. Some ignorantly think, that because they are poor in the world, and their lot very hard they will surely be well in another world. O deceive not yourselves. As God has no regard to men's riches in saving them, he has as little regard to their poverty: but be they poor or rich, if they be not in Christ, new creatures, really godly, they will be ruined for ever, John iii. 3; Exod. xxiii. 3.

6*thly*, Believing the great promise of the gospel with application to yourselves, Heb. viii. 10, "This is the covenant that I will make with the house of Israel after those days, saith the Lord; I will be to them a God, and they shall be to me a people, Hos. ii. 19, "And I will betroth thee unto me for ever, yea, I will betroth thee unto me in righteousness, and in judgment, and in loving kindness, and in mercies." Your crosses in the world may well be taken by you for an alarm, saying, Depart, here is not your rest. God is setting fire to the nests you would build to yourselves among the things of the world; and withal holding out to you the great promise of the gospel. O embrace it, and trust him in it, Zeph. iii. 12. And thus shall ye defeat the frowning world effectually. Believing God to be your God in Christ, ye will be very easy whether the world smile or frown, Hab. iii. 17.

Lastly, Believing, that, through the grace of Christ Jesus, even the frowns of the world shall be turned to your good: Rom. viii. 28, " We know," says the apostle, " that all things work together for good, to them that love God, to them who are the called according to his purpose." How often has honey been gotten out of the carcas of the lion, and much good found to grow within a thorn-hedge of afflictions? The cross has brought forth much good fruit in them that have been exercised thereby: and God is kind to you indeed, if you take it so, in that he makes the world so strange to you, that ye may the more seek after acquaintance with him.

Thirdly, The things of the world set out the mixed band of the world's cares. There is none will be free of attacks from these: even a crown is lined with cares. Yea, we must needs care; our daily bread will not drop down into our mouths, nor will our necessary business be managed without thought. But men are in danger by lawful things, and not by unlawful only. And the cares of the world are often ruining unto the soul. They are apt to put the man on a rack, to stretch out one's mind as on tenter-pins, degenerating into a faithless anxiety, Matth. vi. 25, Take no thought; in the Greek it is, Be not racked in your soul; to trouble one so as to unfit him for his duty to God, Luke x. 41; to swallow up all other concerns, and to render the Lord's word, the food of the soul, quite unprofitable, Matth. xiii. 22. Fight in faith against them,

1*st*, Believing that the success of your affairs depends on the blessing of God on your endeavours, not on your anxious care about them; Psal. cxxvii. 1, " Except the Lord build the house, they labour in vain that build it: except the Lord keep the city, the watchman waketh but in vain." The vanity and uselessness of our anxiety may be very plainly read in many experiments; Matthew vi. 27, " Which of you by taking thought can add one cubit unto his stature?" In Providence's management of the world, how often is it seen that the race is not to the swift, nor the battle to the strong, neither yet bread to the wise, nor yet riches to men of understanding, nor yet favour to men of skill, but time and chance happeneth to them all, Eccl. ix.

11; and that by strength no man shall prevail? How often does some unforeseen event render a hopeful and promising project vain? and, on the other hand, set right again what seemed to be quite marred?

2*dly*, Believing that the best way to secure what is truly necessary and fit for you in this world, it is to be first and mainly taken up about the things of another life. Hence says our Lord, Matth. vi. 33, " Seek ye first the kingdom of God, and his righteousness, and all these things shall be added unto you." They that are careful how to please God, God will see to them that they be provided, Psal. xxxiv. 10. They whose main care is for the eternal welfare of their souls, may expect, that, in the use of means, the temporal welfare of their bodies shall be seen to by heaven. This is the shortest and surest way to prosper, Psal. i. 3.

3*dly*, Trusting the Lord with all your concerns which require your care, depending on him as the sovereign manager, and as a sure and safe manager for you. Hence is that exhortation, Psal. xxxvii. 3, " Trust in the Lord, and do good ; so shalt thou dwell in the land, and verily thou shalt be fed." And ye should trust in him both as to your own conduct and success, both for direction and prospering: Prov. iii. 5, 6, " Trust in the Lord with all thine heart; and lean not unto thine own understanding. In all thy ways acknowledge him, and he shall direct thy paths." This implies three things.

(1.) Laying your burden of care over on the Lord himself, believing that he will care for you, 1 Pet. v. 7. Many an unbelieving lift we take of our own burden, and then we complain that we are not able to go under it : but Jesus Christ is appointed to be the great burden-bearer for poor sinners, and they are called to cast their burdens on him, Psal. lv. 22, and xxxvii. 5. If they will needs take their burdens, and keep them on their own shoulders, who can help it? But faith's work is to trust him with all.

(2.) Believing, that he will do the best: Psal. lxxxv. 12, "The Lord shall give that which is good;" xxxiv. 10, " They that seek the Lord, shall not want any good thing." He knows himself what is best for us, we know it not : and we owe to him a faith so far implicit, as to believe whatever God doth is best done ; and whatever way he leads us, that it is best for us to follow, as did Abraham, Heb. xi. 8. It is the property of faith, thus to resign all to the Lord, trusting, that whatsoever is truly best for us, he will bring it about.

(3.) Staying yourself upon the word of the promise, Gen. xxxii. 12, " I will surely do thee good." Thus faith is to be an anchor of the soul in doubtful events. While anxious care leaves a person nothing to fix on, but causeth him to waver like meteors in the air; faith fixeth on the promise of God, and renders the soul easy, come what will, Luke xii. 29; 1 Sam. i. 18.

2dly, The men of the world are dangerous enemies also. There is an old enmity, which will not cease to work in them, Gen. iii. 15. They are agents for the devil, factors for hell, soldiers in pay to fight Satan's battles. No man will get to heaven without a struggle with them; for they are opposite parties to all that really mind to be there. We find David very concerned to be delivered from them, Psal. xvii. 13, 14, "Deliver my soul," says he, "from the wicked, which is thy sword: from men which are thy hand, O Lord, from men of the world, which have their portion in this life, and whose belly thou fillest with thy hid treasure." We likewise find the apostle Paul was so concerned, 2 Thess. iii. 1, 2, "Finally, brethren," says he, "pray for us,—that we may be delivered from unreasonable and wicked men." And our Lord forewarns his disciples of the world's hatred, John xv. 19, "If ye were of the world," says he, "the world would love his own: but because ye are not of the world, but I have chosen you out of the world, therefore the world hateth you." Now, the men of the world manage the battle three ways, viz. (1.) with the tongue, (2.) with their feet, (3.) with their hands; and ye must resist them still one way, viz. in faith.

1. The men of the world fight against the children of God with the tongue. They are the seed of the serpent; and therefore it is no wonder to see them spit their venom against such as go not their way. Hence we read of their "imagining mischiefs in their heart;" of their being "continually gathered together for war;" of their having "sharpened their tongues like a serpent:" of adder's poison being under their lips, Psal. cxl. 2, 3. Ishmael's mocking Isaac, Gen. xxi. 9, is called persecution, Gal. iv. 29. The trial of the believing Hebrews was the reproaches of ungodly men, Heb. x. 32, 33. See what a conspiracy was formed against Jeremiah, Jer. xviii. 18, "Come, said they, and let us devise devices against Jeremiah: for the law shall not perish from the priest, nor counsel from the wise, nor the word from the prophet: come, and let us smite him with the tongue, and let us not give heed to any of his words." See likewise what a secret consultation was formed against David, intimated in that prayer of his, Psal. lxiv. 2, 3, "Hide me from the secret counsel of the wicked; from the insurrection of the workers of iniquity: who whet their tongues like a sword, and bend their bows to shoot their arrows, even bitter words. God's people are to fight in faith in this case,

1st, Believing, that our God is able to blunt the edge of their swords, and the points of their arrows, and will do it so far as he sees meet. Hence is that promise, Job v. 21, "Thou shalt be hid from the scourge of the tongue." It is in the power of their hand to fling dirt upon the faces of God's children; but it is not in their power to cause it to stick, unless the Lord has said it for the greater trial of his people. God has the hearts of all men in his hands, and his people may confidently trust in him with the preserving of their reputation while they keep his way.

2*dly*, Believing that all the dirt a mischevious world flings in the face of the Lord's people, the day will come that God will wipe it cleanly away from off them, and throw it back on the faces of them that cast it: Is. li. 8, "Hearken unto me, ye that know righteousness, the people in whose heart is my law, fear ye not the reproach of men, neither be ye afraid of their revilings. For the moth shall eat them up like a garment, and the worm shall eat them like wool: but my righteousness shall be for ever, and my salvation from generation to generation." A lying tongue is but for a moment, and will rebound upon them that use such a hellish weapon. God has secured by promise the taking away of reproaches from off his people: Psal. xxxvii. 6, "And he shall bring forth thy righteousness, as the light, and thy judgment as the moon-day. lxviii. 13, "Though ye have lien among the pots, ye shall be as the wings of a dove covered with silver, and her feathers with yellow gold." And so, in the faith of the promise, they may be very easy; and considering the use God may have for them for their good, may find soul refreshment in them. Hence says our Lord, Matth. v. 11, 12, "Blessed are ye when men shall revile you, and persecute you, and shall say all manner of evil against you falsely for my sake. Rejoice, and be exceeding glad: for great is your reward in heaven: for so persecuted they the prophets which were before you." And says the apostle, 2 Cor. xii. 10, "I take pleasure in reproaches, in persecutions, in distresses for Christ's sake."

2. The men of the world fight against the children of God with their feet; that is, by the example of their unholy lives. And much mischief they do by that means; hereby heaps are made to lie upon heaps. Hence says our Lord, Matth. xviii. 7, "Woe unto the world because of offences: for it must needs be that offences come: but woe to that man by whom the offence cometh." It is hard to bear up against the course of the world lying in wickedness, to swim against that stream, considering the corruption of nature that is in the best. By the force of ill examples, many good men have been worsted, many that had not the root of the matter in them have been ruined: Matth. xxiv. 13, "And because iniquity shall abound, the love of many shall wax cold." Fight against it in faith,

1*st*, Believing, that the way of the world is the way to eternal ruin: Eph. ii. 2, "Wherein in time past ye walked according to the course of this world, according to the prince of the power of air, the spirit that now worketh in the children of disobedience, Prov. xiii. 20. "A companion of fools shall be destroyed." Are we not expressly told, that the multitude is going in the way to destruction? and that there be very few which are on the way to heaven, Matth. vii. So that whosoever mind for heaven, must needs be nonconformists to the world, though thereby they become the world's wonder, like Joshua and his fellows. See 1 Pet. iv. 4.

2*dly*, Believing, that, through the grace of the Lord Jesus, ye shall be able to stand the shock of the corrupt example of the world. The eye of faith will discern the greater strength to be on the side of the wrestler against ill example. Hence said Elisha, in another case, to his servant, 2 Kings vi. 16, "Fear not: for they that be with us, are more than they that be with them." And says the apostle, 1 John iv. 4, "Ye are of God, little children, and have overcome them: because greater is he that is in you, than he that is in the world. If God be for us, who can be against us?" And for us he will be, if we trust him for our upbearing against it. He strengthens the spoiled against the strong: and be the force of the current never so great, they "can do all things through Christ which strengtheneth them," Philip. iv. 13.

3. The men of the world fight against the children of God with their hands. There is never a wicked man in the world, but, by his natural make and frame, is a persecutor, Gen. iii. 15. And none is fit to travel the road to heaven, but they that are resolute to hold on their way, notwithstanding all the mischief a wicked world may do them. Hence says our Lord, Luke xiv. 26, "If any man come to me, and hate not his father, and mother, and wife, and children, and brethren, and sisters, yea, and his own life also, he cannot be my disciple." Sometimes indeed God binds their hands, that they can do nothing with them against his people; but the mischievous persecuting nature never leaves the serpent's seed: and according as holy providence looseth the cord, so will they vent it. But resist in faith,

1*st*, Believing, that it is little they can do, when they do their worst. Hence says our Lord, Luke xii. 4, 5, "Be not afraid of them that kill the body, and after that, have no more that they can do, But I will forewarn you whom you shall fear; Fear him, which, after he hath killed, hath power to cast into hell; yea I say unto you, fear him." The utmost reach of the most malicious and powerful persecutors, is but to the body, and things that concern time.

And what is the body in comparison of the soul? time-things in comparison of those which are eternal? The faith of this carried up the martyrs, and armed them with a holy contempt of the impotent rage of their persecutors.

2*dly*, Believing that they are ever under the check and control of a gracious God, engaged on the side of those that keep his way: Psal. lxxvi. 10, "Surely the wrath of man shall praise thee: the remainder of wrath shalt thou restrain." So that "he that walketh uprightly, walketh surely, Prov. x. 9. How spitefully did Laban pursue Jacob, and Saul, David? but God put a check on them. Faith will discover in this case an almighty power for protection, and man to be but a worm, a fading thing which shall be like grass, Is. li. 12.

3*dly*, Believing the eternal rest, peace, and safety, that remains for the people of God: 2 Cor. iv. 17, 18, "Our light affliction, which is but for a moment, worketh for us a far more exceeding and eternal weight of glory; while we look not at the things which are seen, but at the things which are not seen: for the things which are seen, are temporal; but the things which are not seen, are eternal." It is but a short time we are to remain among the inhabitants of this world: the firm faith of that, with the faith of a better life, would make us very easy whether we have their smiles or frowns. Our great concern is to fight our way to the better world, and resolutely to cleave to the Lord and the way of duty, over the belly both of the things and the men of the world.

Sixthly, There is a fight of faith with sin: Heb. xii. 4, "Ye have not yet resisted unto blood, striving against sin." Of all things, there is nothing so opposite to God as sin is. The devil brought it into the world at first: and fearful havoc has it made therein, ever since its entrance; destroying the most part of Adam's children, wounding and doing mischief to all. And none can reach heaven, but those who both fight and overcome it: and there is no successful fighting against it, but in faith. And that ye may know what you have to fight against here,

1. There is the Captain of this hellish band; that is the sin of our nature.

2. There is a swarm of hellish lusts, as soldiers under the command of the sin of our nature.

First, There is the captain of this hellish band; that is, the sin of our nature, called "the old man, the flesh, and sin," by the way of eminence, Rom. vi. 12. Sin is woven into our very natures: our nature has got a wrong set by Adam's fall. It is averse to good, and prone to evil; the bias of it lies quite the wrong way. This corrupt disposition is most active, and by its indwelling and activity fights against the soul. And it exerts itself against the soul especially these three ways.

1. With its guilt, whereby it binds over the soul to the anger of God: the soul out of Christ to his revenging wrath, and even the believing soul to fatherly anger and displeasure, Gal. iii. 10; Psal. lxxxix. 30, &c. The conscience feeling the band of sin on it, is frightened and fired. The man sees himself, by reason of the corruption and pollution of his nature, an object of God's indignation, liable to the fearful strokes of his hand: even as a serpent, or any other poisonous creature, is liable to the stroke of a man's hand wherever he meets with it. Now, if ever ye would break these bonds of guilt, fight against them in faith,

1*st*, Believing, that the Lord Jesus Christ has made a complete satisfaction to the justice of God, not only for actual sins, but even for the sin of our nature, Rom. vi. 6, "Knowing this, that our old man is crucified with him, that the body of sin might be destroyed." In respect of the sin of our nature we needed a Saviour; and it was reckoned to him, to be cleared by him, as well as our actual transgressions. So that there is a sufficient remedy provided against the guilt of the sin of our nature, in Jesus Christ; so that no man needs to despond in that case as hopeless.

2*dly*, Believing, embracing, and trusting to the promise of remission of sin through the blood of Christ: Eph. i. 7, "In him we have redemption through his blood; the forgiveness of sins, according to the riches of his grace." While the conscience is fired with guilt, faith must discern the promise of remission through Christ held forth in the gospel, like a rope to drowning men, Luke xxiv. 47. And faith must embrace that promise, relying on it as the Lord's own promise; even as the drowning man ventures his life on the rope let down to him: and so shall that guilt be removed, and the conscience purged, Acts xiii. 38, 39; Rom. iii. 24, 25. Your warrant is, Acts xiii. 38, "Be it known unto you, that through this man is preached unto the you forgiveness of sins."

3*dly*, Believing and applying to yourselves, and pleading the perfect holiness of Christ's birth and nature, as a public person, Col. ii. 10, 11. Thus faith may triumph over the sin of one's nature, as to the guilt of it. While the law says, Thou hast an unholy nature, and therefore must die the death: Yea, may the soul say, True, my nature is unholy in me; but Christ has satisfied for that guilt: and I have a holy nature in Christ, in him as a public person I was born holy, and retain the holiness of nature: and therefore I must not die, but live.

OBJECTION But, alas! I dare not apply Christ's perfect holiness to myself, for I fear I have not right to it. ANSWER. There is a twofold right. (1.) To a thing. (2.) In it. What right has a beggar to a penny which a man seriously holds out to him, saying, Hae, there is a penny? He certainly has a right to that penny: he may lawfully take it out of that man's hand, and put in his pocket. Such a right every one of you has to Christ's righteousness, whereof this is a part. It is God's gift to you Rom. v. 17; John vi. 32; held out to you to be received and applied by faith, Rom. i. 17. If the beggar neglect or refuse it, though he had a right to it, he is justly deprived of it; and the man may put it in his own pocket again: but if he do take it, then he has a right to it; it is his own in possession, and cannot be taken from him again. Go then, and take the gift of righteousness out of Christ's hand, verily believing that ye have a right to it.

2. With its motions and activity, Rom. vii. 5. It is an active principle, still tending to corrupt the soul more, fighting for the throne in the heart, and to cause the soul obey it, in fulfilling its lusts. And it must be fought against, to the breaking of its designs, Rom. vi. 12. It is a restless enemy, present at all times with a man, and especially active at some times, and particularly when one would do good: as it was with Paul, Rom. vii. 21. It is like a dunghill, still sending forth its filthy steams. And as it strives to strengthen itself, and to have the throne; so the Christian must fight against it, to bear it down, weaken, and get it mortified, Gal. v. 17 And ye must for this cause fight in faith against it,

1st. Believing that it is your most dangerous enemy: for so it is indeed. Never did Paul cry out to be delivered from the most bloody men that were set against him, as from indwelling sin, Rom. vii. 24, "O wretched man that I am, who shall deliver me from the body of this death! It is a domestic enemy; an enemy within, more dangerous than all the enemies we have without, whether devils or the present evil world. Were it not for it, they would have a cold coal to blow at. But this furnishes them with notable advantages against us.

2dly, Believing Christ to be the great ordinance of God for sanctification, and looking for your sanctification from him, on the credit of the promise held out in the gospel to you, Is. xlv. 22, "Look unto me, and be ye saved, all the ends of the earth: for I am God, and there is none else." Men have by nature's light been convinced of the necessity of sanctification; and some have thought one means proper to obtain it, and others another. Pagans have thought washings with water, sacrifices, the study of moral virtue, proper means for it. The Jews have added to these the observation of Moses' law, moral, ceremonial, and judicial. The Papists have thought a multitude of uninstituted ceremonies, fastings, whippings, &c. with the work itself in sacraments, all proper to sanctify the unholy. Legalists look on their own faithless endeavours after holiness, their watchings, &c. as proper means to obtain it. But all in vain.

But God has appointed his own Son to be the great ordinance for sanctification of the unholy, that the praise of our sanctification may be his own, as well as of our justification, 1 Cor. i. 30, 31. And he has lodged the fulness of the Spirit of holiness in him, to be partaken of in the way of believing, Acts xxvi. 18. Look how the stung Israelites were cured in the wilderness by looking to the brazen serpent, believing that by that means they should be healed; so is an unholy sinner made holy, looking unto Jesus, trusting unto him for their sanctification, John iii. 14, 15, or as the woman with the bloody issue. Hence the church, believing the promise of sanctification says, Micah vii. 19, "He will turn again, he will have compassion upon us: he will subdue our iniquities: and thou wilt cast all their sins into the depths of the sea."

3*dly*, Struggling against it in the faith of its having got its death's wounds, in the death and resurrection of Christ, as a public person, Rom, vi. 6—9. No wonder they be still under the power of indwelling sin, who struggle against it without an eye to the death of Christ. But the soul by faith eying the death and resurrection of Christ, as the death of sin, will thereby be animated to act against it, like a giant refreshed with wine. The sins of all that are Christ's were imputed to him, and he by his sufferings expiated the guilt of them; and so he rose again free of that imputed guilt: so, in virtue of his death and resurrection, it loses its power over those that are his. And by faith of it, we become partakers of it.

4*thly*, Believing that we shall get the victory over it through Jesus Christ, Rom. viii. 24, 25, "O wretched man that I am, (says Paul); who shall deliver me from the body of this death! I thank God, through Jesus Christ our Lord." They will fight well who are sure of the victory: and it is faith's work to believe the victory over sin, according to the promise, Rom. xvi. 20, "The God of peace shall bruise Satan under your feet shortly." This was included in the first promise, Gen. iii. 15, "The seed of the woman shall bruise the head of the serpent; which was proposed to our first parents to be by them believed.

With its sting still sticking close to the soul, Rom. vii. 17. It cleaves to us, like a stain that cannot be got fully washed off, while we are in this world. It is like the fretting leprosy in the walls of the house, not to be quite removed, till the house be pulled down. Notwithstanding all the struggles against it, it cannot be got to the door till death. Fight in faith against it,

1*st*, Making no truce with it, but ever seeking its ruin, in the faith of Christ's excellency, and sin's hatefulness. The eye of faith fixing on the glory of Christ held forth in the gospel, has a transforming virtue. Hence says the apostle, 2 Cor. ii. 18, "We all with open face, beholding as in a glass the glory of the Lord, are changed into the same image, from glory to glory, even as by the Spirit of the Lord." And thus the heart is separated from sin, and set against it, while yet sin cleaves to the soul. Like the house of David and the house of Saul: no league between them, but the war continued till the house of Saul was quite sunk.

2*dly*, Believing, that the victory over it will be at length full and complete. Resist it in the faith of this. However it appears to be fixed with bands of iron and brass, yet the breaking thereof shall come suddenly, at an instant. As the walls of Jericho fell down on the seventh day, that were not moved while the Israelites compassed them the six days: so at death these walls will fall down, and be razed to the foundation.

Secondly, There is a swarm of hellish lusts as soldiers under the command of the sin of our nature, Rom. vi. 12. These are the members of the old man, the streams flowing from the bitter fountain of the corruption of nature. These "war against the soul," 1 Pet. ii. 11. They seek to drive the soul from God, they push on men to satisfy them with forbidden fruit, and at length drown the soul in destruction and perdition, where they get the final victory, 1 Tim. vi. 9. Against these also ye must fight in faith, resist them, deny them, weaken, mortify, and crucify them.

It is a difficult fight; but faith will help you out in it, as difficult as it is.

1. Their name may be legion, because they are many, Tit. iii. 3. All sin is radically in the corrupt nature of man: and there is never a temptation in the world, but there is in our nature some lust or other akin to it. Look through the world, and see all the abominations which any where appear there some are atheists, adulterers, &c. But the corrupt affections are in every body's heart naturally, Prov. xxvii. 19, "As in water face answereth to face; so the heart of man to man." But resist ye, believing, that, through the grace of the Lord Jesus, the victory is to be got over them all, Psal. cxviii. 12. There is neither strength nor multitude to be feared, where one by faith can oppose to both, the almighty power engaged on the side of the wrestlers against sin. Therefore says the apostle, 2 Tim. ii. 1,

"Thou therefore, my son, be strong in the grace that is in Christ Jesus." The blood of Christ is of infinite value, the Spirit of Christ of infinite efficacy, and faith must rely on these.

2. Their allies are all the powers of hell; Satan, John viii. 44, the world, Tit. ii. 12. All the snares and temptations that are in the world, are allied to some lust of the heart, which answers to them as tinder to fire. But ye should resist, believing that greater is he that is in you, than he that is in that combat, 1 John iv. 4. Oppose to these by faith the divine attributes, his power, wisdom, &c. the name of the Lord, which is a strong tower, &c.

3. Their lodging is not far off. It is the corrupt heart; thence it is that they issue out against us, Mark vii. 21. The heart of man is like a common inn, often so thronged with strangers, that there is no room for the entertainment of the master. But ye must resist them notwithstanding, believing that your helper is as near you as those your enemies, 1 John iv. 4. O it is a trying consideration to a gracious soul to think, that sin is woven into one's very nature, mixed with one's very constitution. But let faith discern the union betwixt Christ and the soul; let the Christian believe that Christ dwells in him by his Spirit, in an indissoluble union; so may he see how to get clear of sin at length.

4. Their qualities are very bad. They are the brats of Babel, the offspring of hell. And,

1*st*, They are greedy and insatiable lusts, Gal. v. 17. They are like the grave and the barren womb, that never say, It is enough. Where they are indulged, and yielded to, they fill the man's hands continually, seeking meat for them, to the provoking of God, Psal. lxxviii. 18; James iv. 3. And the more they are gratified and fed, the more they still crave: so that they "are like the troubled sea, when it cannot rest, whose waters cast up mire and dirt," Is. lvii. 20.

But ye must resist them, if ye mind for heaven. Ye must deny their cravings, Tit. ii. 12. Make no provision for them, but starve them, however painful that may be, Rom. xiii. 14, "But put ye on the Lord Jesus Christ, and make not provision for the flesh, to fulfil the lusts thereof." This is the way to rid yourselves of their trouble; for men's lusts are like fire, that will die out if there be no fuel laid to them.

(1.) Believing, that there is a fulness in Christ, enough to satisfy the soul, to give the heart a complete rest, that it shall need none of those things which nourish lusts, Matth. xiii. 45, 46. The one pearl discovered, stays the pursuit after the many. Hence faith contracts the desires of the soul into one, Psal. xxvii. 4. which is the better part. O what is the cause men are so taken up to satisfy their lusts with their proper food, but the not believing of the fulness of Christ? Psal. iv. 6, 7.

(2.) Embracing that fulness of Christ for, and instead of those things your hearts lust after. This is the import of selling all and buying the field, the one pearl; the soul taking Christ for these things, as in buying one takes the commodity bought instead of all he pays. The surest and shortest way to mortification of lusts is this way of believing, whereby the soul makes a happy exchange; for and instead of such lusts which cleave to him, embracing Christ, from him to draw that content and satisfaction he sought in the lust. Thus men deal with their hearts, as men with children, giving them one thing to get another from them, Rom. xiii. 14. forecited.

(3.) Believing, that you shall find that rest and satisfaction of heart in Christ, which you sought in your lusts. This is the import of the gospel-offer to all, Matth. xi. 28, "Come unto me, all ye that labour, and are heavy laden, and I will give you rest." Is. lv. 1, "Ho, every one that thirsteth, come ye to the waters, and he that hath no money; come ye, buy and eat, yea, come, buy wine and milk without money, and without price." And if you believe it not, you believe not the gospel aright: and always the less ye believe it, the surer gripe will your heart hold of its lusts. But believe it firmly; and the more firmly you believe it, the more will ye let go your gripes of your lusts.

2*dly*, They are hurtful lusts, 1 Tim. vi. 9. And they extend their hurt to the tenderest part of the man, and to the not only wounding, but ruining of it, if the effect thereof be not stopped, destroying the soul. They hurt as water hurteth, drowning the soul, *ibid.*: as fire hurteth, burning it up, Rom. i. 27; as a canker hurteth, eating it away, 2 Tim. ii. 17; as poison hurteth, killing it, Psal cxl. 3; Is. lix. 5. They extend their hurt not only to the party in whose breast they are lodged, but to others, Eccl. ix. 18, "One sinner destroyeth much good." Sometimes one's lust involves many in guilt, and many in trouble; like a fire breaking out in a house, burning down the houses nearest it, and putting all into trouble and vexation. Thus Achan's lust involved his whole family in guilt, and troubled all Israel. Adam's lust ruined all the world.

Ye must therefore beware of them, and of the hurt by them. But deceive not yourselves, thinking ye may entertain them, and not be hurt by them; that ye can take the serpent in your bosom, and not be stung thereby, Prov. vi. 27, 28; Eccl. x. 8. Resist the beginnings of your lusts, nip them in the bud. The longer they go on, they will be the harder to master, like a fire, or a water. If they have got up upon you, by all means endeavour to hinder their spreading; and speedily quench them, if they are spread. To do it to purpose, do it in faith,

(1.) Putting yourself under the divine protection, by trusting in the shadow of the wings of a God in Christ. This is the work of faith. Hence says Boaz to Ruth, chap. ii. 12, " The Lord recompense thy work, and a full reward be given thee of the Lord God of Israel, *under whose wings thou art come to trust.*" This has the promise of protection, Psal. xci. 1, &c. Faith sees the hazard the soul is in from hurtful lusts, and therefore disposeth the soul to all due precaution, and to put the soul in the Lord's hand for keeping, as the chickens get in under the wings of the hen, Psal. xxxi. 5.

(2.) Applying the Redeemer's blood for purging away the guilt brought on the soul by these lusts, Rom. iii. 25; Heb. ix. 14. This is the only way to remove the hurt of them in that case. Thus the hurt of the guilt of them shall be cured, Mark xvi. 17, 18. The guilt of them casts the conscience into a fever; but faith applying the blood of Christ held out in the promise of the gospel, obtains pardon of the guilt, and cools the sick conscience, Is. xxxiii. 24. The access to this blood is free to all, Zech. xiii. 1, " In that day there shall be a fountain opened to the house of David, and to the inhabitants of Jerusalem, for sin, and for uncleanness. 1 Cor. vi. 11, " And such were some of you: but ye are washed, but ye are sanctified, but ye are justified in the name of the Lord Jesus, and by the Spirit of our God."

(3.) Trusting to the fulness of the Spirit of sanctification in Christ, for breaking the power of these lusts, 1 Cor. i. 30. We are not man enough for the least of these powers of hell: therefore we are to trust to borrowed strength, 2 Tim. ii. 1, " Thou therefore, my son, be strong in the grace that is in Christ Jesus." And going out against them in the name of the Lord, like David with his sling, we shall do valiantly: for he "strengtheneth the spoiled against the strong; so that the spoiled shall come against the fortress," Amos v. 9. Thus many who have long been a prey to their lusts, like dead men lying in the grave to the worms, receiving the Spirit of life from Jesus Christ, have shook them off. " For," says the apostle, " the law of the Spirit of life, in Christ Jesus, hath made me free from the law of sin and death," Rom. viii. 2. And in them has been fulfilled in a spiritual sense, Is. xiv. 2, " The people shall take them, and bring them to their place : and the house of Israel shall possess them in the land of the Lord, for servants and handmaids: and they shall take them captives, whose captives they were, and they shall rule over their oppressors." And this in virtue of that, Psal. lxviii. 18, "Thou hast ascended on high, thou hast led captivity captive."

3*dly*, They are restless lusts; "like the troubled sea, that cannot rest, Is. lvii. 20. They are like the midges in a summer day, ever in motion, working some annoyance to the soul. For temptations are thick in the world, and they never want something to stir them up, they are warring lusts, they are never at peace, they are ever in the field of battle.

(1.) Warring among themselves, one against another, Jam. iv. 1. And the soul of man is what they are warring for, which shall possess it, and be governor of it. In this respect the poor sinner's heart is like a town situated in the confines of the territories of several ambitious princes, which is tossed and harrassed amongst them, he fightng to have it, and he fighting to have it; one turning out another, &c. Thus pride and ambition draw the mind one way, covetousness draws him another way: contrary lusts at once fight in him. And there is no peace for the man, but by mortifying both the contending parties.

(2.) They war against the soul, 1 Pet. ii, 11. All of them are enemies to it, and seek its ruin. Though they be contrary one to another, yet they conspire together for the destruction of the soul; like Herod and Pontius Pilate against Christ. The soul, in respect of its make and constitution, is most allied to heaven, and therefore is the special object of their rage.

Wherefore ye also, if ye mind for heaven, must lay your accounts with a continual warfare. Ye must never let down your watch, nor lay by your armour, but ever stand in a fighting posture, Eph. vi. 14, "Stand therefore, having your loins girt about with truth," &c. As there is no peace to be made betwixt contrary lusts, so ye must not side with any of the parties, nor be at peace with either, but maintain the fight against both. And fight in faith,

[1.] Believing that this war will have a comfortable end at length, and ye shall have a profound, perfect, lasting peace, 2 Tim. iv. 7, 8. Though the war with your lusts must be a lasting one; it is good news, that it will not be everlasting; but the peace obtained through the complete victory will be so. Take courage, O Christian, the last stroke will be given ere long in this battle, which will be the decisive stroke. The day will come, when the enemies "ye have seen to-day, ye shall see them again no more for ever, Exod. xiv. 13. In heaven ye will get eternal peace and rest, Rev

xxi. 5. There the centinels are called from their posts, and the men of war lay by their swords, and put on their crowns.

[2.] Believing that your helper is ever as ready as your enemies, Psal. xvi. 8. It is a weighty consideration, that Satan walks about as a roaring lion, seeking whom he may devour, and our enemies within are restless. But faith wants not a solid relief to oppose unto this, looking to the promise, Psal. cxxi. 4, "Behold, he that keepeth Israel, shall neither slumber nor sleep, Is. xxvii. 3, "I the Lord do keep it, I will water it every moment; lest any hurt it, I will keep it night and day." At what time soever the enemies attack us, we may have access to our help: and the faith of the promise will fetch it in as quickly as by a look, Is. xlv. 22, "Look unto me, and be ye saved, all the ends of the earth: for I am God, and there is none else.

[3.] Believing that his grace is ever sufficient for you, 2 Cor. xii. 9. Though the war last long, the stock of strength cannot be wasted, in which ye must fight; since it is an inexhaustible treasure in Christ Jesus, to which ye can never come amiss, John i. 16. Indeed, if ye fight in your own strength, ye will soon find it wasted: but faith's work is to fetch in strength from Christ, and it is sufficient for the continued warfare, Is. xl. 31.

Lastly, They are deceitful lusts, Eph. iv. 22. We are apt to be beguiled by them, if we take not good heed. They deceive sinners, and then take them captive, Tit. iii. 3; and then slay them, Rom. vii. 11. They are the golden cup in Satan's hand, by which he ministers poison to the soul. They are deceitful: for,

(1.) They always promise what they never perform, 2 Pet. ii. 19. Who is the man that is not disappointed in them looking for that content and satisfaction he never finds? How was Judas deceived that way?

(2.) They often commend themselves to men under the mask of some harmless thing, or some real virtue, Col. ii. 18. Thus, like Satan, they transform themselves into an angel of light. So many call evil good, and good evil, &c.

(3.) There is a hidden mischief in them, when they are most smiling. There is a hook always, which is covered with the bait, James i. 14, "Every man is tempted, when he is drawn away of his own lusts, and enticed." It is a metaphor taken from fishes caught by the bait, and drawn out of the water. But,

Ye must have your eyes in your head, and not be ignorant of Satan's devices, Prov. xxii. 3. Be not rash, but try ere ye trust. Forbidden fruit may be fair to look at, and the devil's ground may be very smooth; and the sinner see no hazard where death is at his elbow, Prov. xiv. 12. Therefore fight as against a deceitful enemy, Eph. xiv. 11. And fight in faith,

[1.] Believing the testimony of God concerning the heart, Jer. xvii. 9, that it is "deceitful above all things, and desperately wicked, who can know it? and therefore keeping a watchful eye, a holy jealousy over it: Prov. xxviii. 14, "Happy is the man that feareth always: but he that hardeneth his heart, shall fall into mischief." Faith is the soul's going out of itself to the Lord, and brings off the man from leaning to his own understanding, Prov. iii. 5, and trusting to his own heart, Prov. xxviii. 26. For these are the things that betray a man into the hands of deceitful lusts.

[2.] Trusting to the conduct of the Lord Jesus Christ, Prov. iii. 6. He is the Captain of salvation, the appointed leader of his people, eyes to them in the wilderness. And he will teach those who are willing to be taught, Psal. xxv. 9. And there is no way to get clear of the deceitful lusts, but by shutting our own eyes, and looking to the Lord for light to discern our way. For he is made wisdom for us, 1 Cor. i. 30, and by faith in him, "the way-faring men, though fools, shall not err in the way of holiness," Is. xxxv. 8.

Lastly, There is a fight with death. This is the last enemy ye will have to grapple with: 1 Cor. xv. 26, "The last enemy that shall be destroyed, is death." There was never any who escaped this combat, but Enoch and Elias. As for all others, the encounter with it is appointed of Heaven, Heb. ix. 27. And there is no freeing of any from this battle, Eccl. viii. 8. Many trouble not themselves to fight with temptation, or with sin, but live at peace with these their enemies: but, whether they will or not, they must feel the bitterness of death. If ever ye would fight it so as to overcome, ye must fight in faith. Here consider,

1. How death may attack you; and,
2. In what shapes it may do so.

1*st*, How death may attack you. And that,

First, With sorrow and heaviness, Psal. cxvi. 3. Death is apt to let in a flood of sorrows upon poor sinners: so that those who have spent their days in mirth, find then all their mirth quite swallowed up in that flood; and they who have had a life of sorrows, feel then the flood of them swelling to the brim. And there are two sluices death opens to let in this flood.

1. The separation of the man from this world, and all things in it, Is. xxxviii. 11. It comes to carry the man off from this world; to separate betwixt him and his nearest relations; to put an end to any portion of his under the sun, that he shall no more see the sun rise or set again, and have no more access to his own house, or bed, or

board. This is apt to let in a flood of sorrow upon the man. And there is no way to hold out against it, but one of these two;

1st, By turning it into the matter of joy: like those mentioned in Job iii. 22, "which rejoice exceedingly, and are glad when they can find the grave;" when the man is so wearied of the world, that his heart leaps for joy, when God's messenger, death, knocks at his door.

2dly, By a Christian resignation to the will of the Lord, Luke ii. 29, the man being ready calmly to deliver up unto the hands of God, all he has here.

Now, if ye would fight death's sorrows on this head, viz. separation from the world, either of these ways; ye must do it in faith,

(1.) Believing, that, through the alone merits of Christ, ye shall be admitted into a better world, set down in a better house, at a better table, and lie better, even in Abraham's bosom, 2 Tim. vi. 7, 8. Nothing else will work the soul into that Christian resignation. The heart of man will never be truly content to give away this world's good things, while it has no comfortable prospect of better: and therefore Christian resignation at death, will be according to faith's view of better things in the other world, Heb. xi. 13.

(2.) Trusting the same Lord Jesus with the charge and care of those whom ye are to leave and are concerned for, 1 Pet. v. 7, "Casting all your care upon him, for he careth for you." With an eye to this, the Lord has made that promise, Jer. xlix. 11, "Leave thy fatherless children, I will preserve them alive; and let thy widows trust in me." Ungodly men can have no such comfort, in the abundance they have to leave theirs, as a godly man may have in this way of believing, Heb. xi. 22.

2. The separation of the soul from the body, Is. xxxviii. 13, 14. The soul and body are closely knit; but death comes to loose the silver cord that knits them together; like a whirlwind to separate them, and carry them far asunder. The soul has a sure prospect of a separate state, which it has no experience of; and the consideration thereof is apt to fill it with sorrow, on the account of its foreseen widowhood.

There is no making head against this, but in faith;

1st, Believing the soul's union with Jesus Christ, and with God through him, Rom. viii. 38, 39. Thus the soul has full comfort against the separation that death makes. Though the man's spirit parts with his body, yet the Spirit of God still dwells in the soul. God would have his people believe this particularly: and for that cause he has appointed the sacraments, signifying and sealing their union with Christ.

2dly, Believing and trusting for the blessed resurrection of the body at God's appointed time, Job xix. 26. It stays the sorrow of friends at their parting, that they look to meet again in peace: and when the soul and body are parting, the stronger the faith of the joyful resurrection is, the less will the sorrow be on that head. And all that are Christ's have good ground for it: for our Lord has said, John xi. 25, "I am the resurrection, and the life: he that believeth in me, though he were dead, yet shall he live."

Secondly, Death may attack you with fear and terror. Death is of all terrors the most terrible. Hence we read of being "brought to the king of terrors, Job. xviii. 14. And therefore the scripture expresseth the greatest consternation by the terrors of death; as in the case of David, Psal. lv. 4, "The terrors of death are fallen upon me." And says Job, chap. xxiv. 17, "For the morning is to them even as the shadow of death: if one know them, they are in the terrors of the shadow of death." Death will appal and damp the stoutest heart: it will fill them with fear, who have been a terror to others in the land of the living. But faith will bear out, where natural courage falls like a dyke of sand before a sweeping flood. Now, there are three sources of the terrors of death.

1. Guilt lying on the soul, 1 Cor. xv. 56, "The sting of death is sin." By the guilt of sin, the sinner is bound over to death; so that is the sting wherewith it pierces men. The native guilt of sin binds over the sinner to death in its full extent, even to revenging wrath: the moderated guilt of it binds over the sinner to unstinged death. When death comes up, it takes the man prisoner as a guilty man; and so fills him with terror. Here must be a close fight of faith to stop this source of fear and terror.

1*st*, Over the belly of all your doubts, fears, and felt unworthiness, stretching out the hand of faith, and laying it on the head of the great sacrifice Christ, and so transferring all your guilt on him, Rom. iii. 25, and v. 11. Ye must believe in, and trust on the obedience and death of Christ, for the removal of your guilt; believing, that, for the sake of a crucified Christ, all your sins shall be pardoned. And for the warrant of your so trusting, ye must discern the pardon offered to you through Christ in the gospel, Acts xii. 38, 39; and so, amidst all your doubts and fears, anchor your souls on the faithfulness of God in the promise. Thus ye shall pull out death's sting, obtaining the removal of guilt by faith in his blood.

2*dly*, Believing and applying to yourselves Christ's full answering of the demands of the law, whereby the law is disarmed of its curse, and the bond of it as a covenant is loosed from off you, Gal. ii. 20; Col. ii. 14. Death's strength lies in guilt: take away guilt off the soul, death is like Samson without his hair. The strength of guilt lies in the law as a covenant: remove the bond of the law from off the man, and the man's guilt is like the cords the Philistines bound Samson with, which became as flax burnt with fire, Judg. xvi. 14. Let faith apply to the soul Christ's obedience and death, and so his fully answering the demands of the law: and then the law can have no more effect on you, than a subscribed bond fully paid and discharged, blotted and rent in pieces, can have on you.

2. The unseen unknown world, therefore called the land of darkness, Job x. 21. One is apt to be seized with fear, when they are to be carried into a place which they do not know. Death comes to carry us to another world, which we never saw, nor can see till we be there, never to come back: and that makes it terrible. It is the world of spirits: the blessed spirits dwelling in the upper regions; the damned spirits in the lower. We are so unacquainted with the inhabitants of that world, that the sight of a spirit, good or bad, would be enough to frighten us while we are here: what wonder then that death be terrible, coming to carry us, where there are none but spirits? Here is great necessity of faith, to bear up against the fear rising from thence. We must then stay our hearts by faith,

1*st*, Firmly believing the scripture accounts of the unseen world, Heb. xi. 1. Though we have never seen it, yet we have heard of it: though we never were there, yet the map of it has been laid before us in the Bible; and there we have it described both the upper and lower part of it. And in that map, drawn by inspired pens, not capable of erring, the lower part of that world is not more dreadful, than the upper part is pleasant and desirable, John xiv. 2; Rev. xxi. The faith of heaven is staying to the heart in some measure.

2*dly*, Firmly believing the scripture account of the way to heaven; that Christ is the way to it, John xiv. 6; and that by faith we walk in him to it, Col. ii. 6. If we believe not this, our hearts have nothing to stay themselves on, but are left at an utter uncertainty, in our encounter with death. Therefore labour to strengthen your faith of this, that it may not be yea and nay, but yea with you, 2 Cor. i. 19, 20; that "he that believeth, shall be saved."

3*dly*, Believing in the Lord Jesus Christ, for your safe passage to the upper part of the unseen world, Psal. lxxiii. 24, and xxxi. 5; committing your soul to him, rolling the weight of your through-bearing on him as the Captain of salvation appointed of God to bring many sons to glory. Take hold of him, by his word of promise, by the everlasting covenant, 2 Sam. xxiii. 5; and labour to gripe some particular promise for that end, as Is. xliii. 2, "When thou passest through the waters, I will be with thee; and through the rivers, they shall not overflow thee: when thou walkest through the fire, thou shalt not be burnt; neither shall the flame kindle upon thee." Heb. xiii. 5, "I will never leave thee, nor forsake thee." Is. xxxv. 9, 10, "No lion shall be there, nor any ravenous beast shall go up thereon, it shall not be found there: but the redeemed shall walk there. And the ransomed of the Lord shall return and come to Zion with songs, and everlasting joy upon their heads: they shall obtain joy and gladness, and sorrow and sighing shall flee away."

4thly, Believing that your Lord Christ is Lord of the unseen world, and that the whole compass of it above and below is under his dominion, Rev. i. 18. It is in his hand that the disposing of souls to any part of that world is. Neither is he to fight with the prince of darkness, on that side, about any soul. That fight of his with Satan was in this world. When one comes there, the devil cannot touch him, unless given up to him as an executioner. And he has said it, that none that believe in him shall be damned, Mark xvi. 16. Believe it with application.

5thly, Believing, that as soon as your soul departs out of your body, God will receive it into his own hand, Psal. xxxi. 5. compared with Luke xxiii. 46. So David believed, Psal. xxiii. 4, "Yea, though I walk through the valley of the shadow of death, I will fear no evil: for thou art with me, thy rod and thy staff they comfort me." It shall be conducted by angels into Abraham's bosom, Luke xvi. 22. Believe, that the same God who brought thee out of the womb, safe into this world, when thou wast a naked helpless infant, and by his providence preserved thee, will take the same care of thee, when entering into the unseen world. This is the comfort of faith in death; agreeably to what the Psalmist saith, Psal. xxii. 9, 10, "But thou art he that took me out of the womb; thou didst make me hope, when I was upon my mother's breasts. I was cast upon thee from the womb: thou art my God from my mother's belly."

Lastly, That thy God will fit thee both for the place and the company, however unfit thou art for them now, Heb. xii. 23. He will do it in a moment, as appears from parity of reason from 1 Cor. xv. 51, 52, "Behold, I show you a mystery; We shall not all sleep, but we shall all be changed, in a moment, in the twinkling of an eye," &c. Believe that he will fit thee, not only for the sight or knowledge of the spirits there before thee, but for communion with them. And thou mayst confirm thy faith of this, by the experience thou hast had (1.) of his fitting thee for communion with the inhabitants of this world, though thou camest into it an infant knowing nobody there, no not the mother that bare thee; and (2.) of his fitting thee for communion with himself, though thou wast by nature dead in sin.

3. The judgment, Heb. ix. 27. The appearing before a tribunal

is an awful thing. When a guilty creature is lying on a death-bed, drawing his last breath, and considers that in a little he is to be carried before his judge in another world, to be judged, and give account of his deeds done in the body, and to receive his sentence for eternity, in well or woe; no wonder fear and terror seize him. There is no making head against this but by faith,

1*st*, Receiving and embracing the Lord Jesus Christ, with all his salvation offered to you in the gospel, John i. 12. So in Rev. xxii. 17, the offer of Christ is made, after the warning given of Christ's coming to judgment: for this only is the way how a sinner may stand before him. While a sinner breathes in this world, he is in the way: and that is the time to agree with the adversary. Christ and all his salvation is offered; that is, pardon, peace, right to glory, sanctification, &c. And it is the work of faith to receive them, held forth in the gospel-promise.

For this cause it is necessary to judge ourselves, and condemn ourselves; to call over all our bypast life, with the sin of our nature: and renouncing all confidence in ourselves, to fly to the horns of the altar, confiding in a crucified Christ, upon the ground of God's faithfulness in the promise of the gospel; John iii. 16, "For God so loved the world, that he gave his only begotten Son, that whosoever believeth in him, should not perish, but have everlasting life."

2*dly*, Believing, that the same Jesus who is offered, and whom you have embraced, in the gospel, is the judge whom you are to appear before, John v. 22, "For the Father judgeth no man; but hath committed all judgment unto the Son." This is a fit means to abate the terror of the judgment-seat to a believer. For thus, by the eye of faith, the soul may see, that it is the very same person who is its head, husband, advocate, and the redeemer, who is its judge. And thus a full fountain of consolation is opened against the terrors of death, arising from the judgment.

3*dly*, Believing, that you being in Christ, judgment will not proceed upon you according to the law of works, but according to the law of faith, *i. e.* the covenant of grace, Rev. xx. 12. The law of works adjudgeth every one that sins in the least to die, Gen. ii. 17; Gal. iii. 10; and according to it shall all unbelievers be judged; but no believer, Rom. vi. 14. The covenant of grace adjudgeth every soul united to Christ by faith, how many soever his sins have been, to live eternally, for the sake of Christ's obedience and death imputed to him, Rom. viii. 1; John iii. 16.

Lastly, Believing, that the covert of Christ's blood is a perfect covert, within which not one drop of revenging wrath can fall here or hereafter, Is. xxxii. 2; and that faith's plea will never be rejected, for it is established by the covenant betwixt the Father and the Son, and God's faithfulness is impawned for it. Let the believer then, thinking on the tribunal, behold the rainbow about the throne, Rev. iv. 3. compared with Is. liv. 9. and be comforted against the terror of death from this quarter.

Thirdly, With despondency, Lam. iii. 18. This is the most fearful weapon wherewith death attacks a man; when it goes about to raise a man's hope in Christ, making his heart to sink within him as hopeless, filling him with a fearful expectation of eternal destruction, Job xxxiii. 22. This may be the case of those that are strangers to Christ, whom death seizing after a lifetime spent in profanity and wickedness, their sins, especially their gross heaven-daring abominations staring them in the face while they are death's prisoners, are apt to fill them with despair of mercy, Job xviii. 14. It may also be the case of saints after a careless untender walk, Psal. lxix. 2, lxxvii. 7; Matth. xxv. 5. Here is need of faith in a special manner,

1st, Believing with application the infinite efficacy of the blood and Spirit of Christ Jesus, Heb. vii. 25. The soul would behold that blood as the blood of the Son of God, 1 John i. 7, and therefore of infinite efficacy to do away the greatest guilt; as the sea, to quench a house on fire, as well as a candle: his Spirit is of infinite efficacy, as able to wipe away the deepest stains of sins, as others, 1 Cor. vi. 11: a water-flood, sweeping away whole dunghills, as well as mole-hills.

2dly, Believing that ye are still within the compass of the gospel offer, Is. lv. 1; Rev. xxii. 17. Yea, it is directed to you in particular, as Jer. iii. 1, "Thou hast played the harlot with many lovers; yet return again to me, saith the Lord." Is. i. 18, "Come now and let us reason together, saith the Lord: though your sins be as scarlet, they shall as white as snow; though they be red like crimson, they shall be as wool." God has made no exception of sinners of any size, who will come in; though ordinarily a profane graceless life has a disagreeable end; they that live gracelessly, for the most part dying hardened, sometimes in sullen despondency: yet the case of the thief on the cross, shews a possibility of its being otherwise.

Lastly, Believing, griping, and hanging by the promise of the gospel, over the belly of all objections, Acts xvi. 21. Though you are in a boisterous sea, where one wave comes after another to sweep you away; yet quit not your gripe, Heb. x. 39; but hope against hope, as Abraham did; for it is pleasing to God, Psal. cxlvii. 11, and will have a good issue, as in the woman of Canaan.

2dly, Consider in what shapes death may attack us. There is one way of coming into the world, but there are many ways of going out of it. Which of them may be ours, we know not: and therefore it concerns us to be ready to encounter death, and fight the last battle successfully, in whatever shape death come upon us. I will take notice of these four.

1. A violent death, by the hands of men. This the heaviest of deaths, when it is an ill cause; as in the case of malefactors, by the hand of public justice; and of men falling sacrifices to their own and others rage in their private godless quarrels. All I say to that, is, to advise you to live by faith, that ye may be preserved from such a death, Prov. xxviii. 17; Matth. xxvi. 52. But even in a good cause men may be brought to it, whether more solemnly by process of law, or summarily by the hands of bloody men. Death in that shape must be fought,

1*st*, Believing that that was the kind of death which Christ died, and so has sanctified it to his own, that they may comfortably venture on it for his sake and cause. And the saints of the highest class have died so, dying martyrs, in numberless multitudes. Our Lord will have all his to lay their accounts with it, Luke xiv. 26, "If any man come to me," says he, "and hate not—his own life, he cannot be my disciple;" though he does not call them all to it. But many who have been called to it have rejoiced in it as their honour.

2*dly*, Believing that great truth with application, Matth. xvi. 25. "Whosoever shall save his life, shall loose it: and whosoever will lose his life for my sake shall find it." When one's life comes in competition with the honour of Christ and the cause of truth, and they will, for saving themselves, make shipwreck of faith and a good conscience; they lose their souls, to save their bodies for a little time: whereas they to whom Christ's honour is more dear than their own lives, their souls shall be saved eternally, and eternal glory will more than make make up all their losses.

2. A painful death. Death in any shape can hardly want pain; but death is certainly more painful to some than to others. O what piercing pains, gripes, and torments, do some suffer at their death! What struggles and wrestlings have some with death, before their souls leave their bodies! What measure of these pains is allotted to us we do not know; but every one will at length feel his own part of them.

Our business is to bear them Christianly and patiently; and that we will never do to purpose, but by faith,

1*st*, Cleaving to Christ in them by faith, Job xiii. 15, and believing, that through his grace they shall have a comfortable end in due time, 2 Tim. iv. 6, 7, 8. Faith's view of the eternal rest in heaven, is the best cordial in the pain of death. When the soul believes, that the last pain is coming up, the last sob; after which sorrow and sighing shall for ever fly away; that will make the man stand the shock of the sharpest pains Christianly and patiently.

2*dly*, Believing that the body of death and sin, which thou hast had many a battle with in thy life, is by that means to be put to the door. Death came in by sin, and sin must go out by death. Every pain and gripe looseth a pin of the tabernacle; and according as death makes its progress in the believer's body, sin is the nearer to a removal out of his soul. And when death has perfected its work on the body, the soul shall then be perfected, Heb. xii. 23. A Christian will abide sore thrusts patiently, in the faith of this their thrusting out his worst enemy.

3*dly*, By the eye of faith discerning death unstinged to thee, by the death of Christ. Our Lord Christ has said it, and done it, Hos. xiii. 14, " I will ransom thee from the power of the grave: I will redeem them from death: O death I will be thy plagues; O grave, I will be thy destruction; repentance shall be hid from mine eyes:" and therefore a dying saint should comfort himself in it, and believing sing, as in 1 Cor. xv. 55—57, " O death, where is thy sting? O grave where is thy victory? The sting of death is sin; and the strength, of sin is the law. But thanks be to God, which giveth us the victory through our Lord Jesus Christ." That whereby the believer's dying body is pained, is not death's sting: he may therefore bear it the better. Death's sting stings the soul and conscience, and leaves the venom of the curse there, which will scorch the man eternally. These pains are but as a bee-sting in comparison of that.

3. A longsome or lingering death. Death makes quick harvest with some, but with others death's work is spun out to a great length; whereby they have many deaths in one, are often looking for the last stroke, but it is long a coming. This is a great trial, and we know not but it may be ours. Therefore we should be prepared for it, and lay up timely for it. We will never manage it well, but by faith,

1*st*, Believing always that it is coming; but at what hour, we know not. The faith of this will make us keep up our watch, Matth. xxiv. 42. They may watch at first, who may let down their watch when they find the Bridegroom delays his coming; and so they may be surprised, as the foolish virgins when their lamps were out. But the faith of this will put us on Job's resolution, chap. xiv. 14, " All the days of my appointed time will I wait till my change come."

2*dly*, Believing that therein the Lord has you upon your trials, 1 Pet. i. 6, 7. He is in that case taking a trial of your faith, love, patience, and Christian fortitude. And if God opens to any of us a scene of trial of more variety and greater length than that of others, it is our business to behave well in the trial laid to our hand.

3*dly*, By the eye of faith discerning the eternal weight of glory, on the other side of the trial: and if we weigh the one by the other, the most longsome struggle with death will appear both light and momentary, 2 Cor. iv. 17, 18, "For our light affliction, which is but for a moment, worketh for us a far more exceeding and eternal weight of glory; while we look not at the things which are seen, but at the things which are not seen: for the things which are seen, are temporal; but the things which are not seen, are eternal."

4. *Lastly*, A sudden death. Death sometimes makes a wide step, so that it is upon a man ere he can well perceive it coming. It is what may be our lot; for it is common to good and bad. Good Eli died so, as well as Ananias and Sapphira, who died with a lie in their mouth. And therefore it concerns us to be prepared for it; which we can never be but by believing. And,

1*st*, Securing ourselves within the true ark, timely, by believing in the Lord Jesus Christ, accepting him in the offer of the gospel covenant, John i. 12. Then come death when and how it will, we are habitually ready for it: and it shall not be able to loose the marriage-knot cast by faith betwixt Christ and our souls, Rom. viii. 38. &c. If in that case, it come suddenly on us, it shall but waft us over more speedily into Immanuel's land.

2*dly*, Resolutely renewing the actings of faith on Christ, at death's sudden approach, Is. xlv. 22. What a man has done before, he may the more easily do again on a signal given: and a believer may through grace renew his acting of faith, upon death's short warning. If death be sudden, the act of faith, may be as sudden, as reaching in a moment from earth to the highest heavens: and therefore compared to a look.

And thus I have gone through the Christian warfare, even to the last battle. May the Lord thus teach our hands to war, and our fingers to fight.

www.ingramcontent.com/pod-product-compliance
Lightning Source LLC
Chambersburg PA
CBHW020008050426
42450CB00005B/362